1717
Real Pirates

· 1717 ·

Real Pirates

The Untold Story of The Whydah
From slave ship to pirate ship

by Barry Clifford and Kenneth J. Kinkor
with Sharon Simpson
Photography by Kenneth Garrett

NATIONAL GEOGRAPHIC

WASHINGTON, D.C.

GOLFE DU MEXIQUE

MEXIQUE ou NOUVELLE ESPAGNE

PRESQU'ISLE DE IUCATAN

GOLPHE - DE HONDURAS

HONDURAS

Nour. Orleans
Pensacola
B. S. Joseph
Cap S. Blaise
R. S. Pierre
R. S. Martin
Baye du St Esprit
les To...

I. de la Chandeleur
Embouchure du Mississipi
I. de la Balise ou S. Louis

Cap de Nord
B. del Ascention
Rio Bacahica
R. S. Juanes

la Durs R.
de la Trinité
la Maline R.
Rivieres de la madelaine

Baye S. Louis ou S. Bernard
Rio Flores
Rio S. Joseph

Embouchure de Rio Bravo
Rio à Palmas
S. Barthelemie
Rio Hermoso
Pointe S. Steven

Cabo Roxo
I. Lobos
S. Basses de Tuspa
Rio de Tuspa
Rio de los Cazones
Rio de S...
I. de San Pablo

Terre brandue
Terre Talabra

Villa-Rica
Rio Simpolanco

La Veracrux
Castean d'Olva
I. de Sacrifices
Punte de Antonio Sardo
Rocca partida

Prov. D'Alvaredo
R. de Med
R. d'Alvara
R. Apualeo

PROVINCE DE GUAZACOALCO
PROV. DE TABASCO
Tabasco

Medas Darcas
Guasacoalco
Route des Barcos
I. Nicolano
Nuestra Señora de la Victoria
Lac de Xicalanco
Salamanca

la à la Havane
Vera cruz

Route de la Flote de la...

la Bermeja
Las Arenas
Alacranes
Basses de Sisal
Sasilun
I. de Cao
Quio
Sisal
S. Francisco de Campeche
Baye de Campeche
Seibo
Valladolid
Lac de Bacala

ISLE DE COZUMEL

Cap Catoche
Cap Saint Antoine
Cap Coriente

Baye Han...
I. de S. Bona

Tropique du Cancer

Iulax venho
I. de Chetumal
I. Pantoja

Cap des 3 Pointes
Rio Dulce
R. de Peches
Rio Baxo

VERA PAZ

SOCONUSCO
GUATIMALA
Barre d'Itapeque

Triomphe de la Croix
Huachico
Porto de Sal
Porto de Cavallas

I. Guanaia
Guanaja
Cap de Honduras
Rio Guanara
Rio Grande
B. de...

Isles de N...

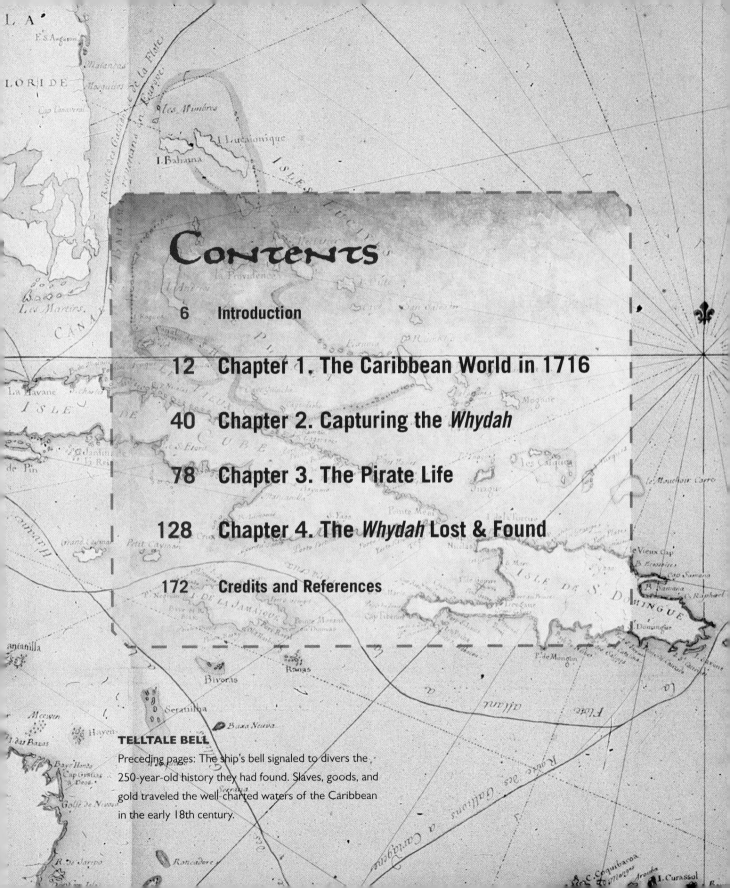

Contents

TELLTALE BELL

Preceding pages: The ship's bell signaled to divers the 250-year-old history they had found. Slaves, goods, and gold traveled the well-charted waters of the Caribbean in the early 18th century.

Introduction

I was not a treasure hunter, although I was obviously hunting for treasure. I was a history hunter, an undersea salvor with a driving interest in bringing a great historic period back to life in a responsible way that an ordinary person could appreciate as well as a historian.

—Barry Clifford

A storm was building in the distant west. I could see it from the deck of the *Vast Explorer.* We were tired, and more than a little disillusioned, from over a year of fruitless searching for the wreck of the pirate ship *Whydah,* rumored to be laden with treasure when it sank off the coast of Cape Cod, Massachusetts, in a tremendous storm in late April 1717.

It had to be there, somewhere off Marconi Beach, but Cape Cod's most enduring legend was proving to be as elusive as the ghost some people said she was.

There was a camera crew aboard that wanted to film us diving. We obliged and sent down a new diver to check the pit—the rest of us were too burned out on that sultry July afternoon in 1984. We had nothing left—our funds were gone, much of our enthusiasm was gone, and, most important, our faith in ourselves was nearly gone as well.

DIVING THE WRECK

Spotlights and metal detectors, together with years of patient diving, have helped Barry Clifford and his dive team salvage the remains of the *Whydah,* a slave ship turned pirate ship, and a story nearly 300 years old.

In less time than it takes to tell it, the diver was back at the surface, tearing at his mouthpiece: "Hey, you guys! There's cannon down there!"

We looked at each other. Our hearts had been broken before. This was the graveyard of the Atlantic, and the "cannon" could just as well be iron from one of the Marconi towers that had tumbled from the sandy Cape Cod clifftops years before, or dummy World War II bombs from the days when the site was a firing range. Still …

Another diver went down. Progressive ear damage from too much diving kept me out of the water. Back he came with a big grin on his face, holding up a small, round object, encrusted in a nearly indistinguishable mass of sand, rock, and grit.

We tapped the object gently with a hammer, and it broke open to reveal a cannonball. I looked inside the molding of oceanbed material that had formed around it. Something that looked like a silver seashell caught my attention. It was a coin. From its markings and shape, it looked like a piece of eight. I flipped it over, and there was a Spanish cross and the date: 1684.

We had done it. We had found the *Whydah.*

I'm often asked what that moment was like—how it felt to have finally found the first pirate shipwreck ever discovered and authenticated.

Moments of discovery are not easy to describe; the words "elation" and "unrestrained joy" come to mind. Certainly it was a soaring moment. I felt like I was atop a mountain, breathing in pure oxygen. We had all worked so long and so hard, and had experienced so much sacrifice and disappointment in the long, hard months of diving for the *Whydah,* but now all of that was gone in the twinkling of a moment.

Much long and hard work, sacrifice, and disappointment lay ahead.

Long John Silver spoke rightly about treasure when he said, "Beware of squalls when you find it." But that was yet to come … as would come other moments of discovery in the quarter century that we've been working the remarkable site.

The treasures of the *Whydah*—gold and silver, coins, weaponry, nautical equipment, 18th-century finery, as well as everyday objects—are spread over a wide area of ocean bottom, blanketed by sand ranging from 10 to 30 feet

HISTORY HUNTER

Barry Clifford takes the helm of *Vast Explorer*, the exploration vessel used regularly to comb the Cape Cod waters for more artifacts from the *Whydah*.

deep. Our continuing work of underwater archaeological discovery is neither easy nor predictable.

As recently as the 2006 season we found a new section of the debris field—and 15 more cannon, which tumbled out of the capsizing wreck. They are lying on top of what appears to be a veritable mountain of other artifacts, yet to be rescued and conserved.

Concealed for years by the magnetic signature from an ill-advised coffer-dam installed at the insistence of an archaeologist, we now find that we still have years of recovery work ahead.

This work will bring new discoveries. Indeed, many of our most exciting finds occur not in the field but in the laboratory, as our technicians and conservators work to clean, conserve, and study the artifacts that have emerged from the ocean floor after centuries.

So it was with the discovery of the ship's bell, which positively identified our wreck as the *Whydah*. So it was with our discovery of the remains of John King—a youngster no older than 11—who joined Capt. Samuel Bellamy's pirate crew despite the desperate pleas of his mother. So it was with our discovery of a pewter plate with an extraordinarily mysterious symbol crudely inscribed on its rim by a pirate.

Each shipwreck is a time capsule, and each artifact from the *Whydah* has its own story to tell about what life was like on April 26, 1717.

Carrying the choice plunder from more than 50 other vessels, the *Whydah* collection represents a priceless sampling of cross-cultural material from the 18th-century world and beyond. It is a unique touchstone to another place and time.

To that end, I am honored by the opportunity to bring this collection to a larger audience to be experienced firsthand.

Discovery is not just about learning new things. It also involves discarding old misconceptions. Preconceptions about pirates abound. One of the most enduring icons of popular culture, the figure of the pirate stands larger than life. As our projects historian, Ken Kinkor, puts it, "the image of the pirate is clouded by the mists of myth and myopia."

Since secrecy was critical to survival, and since pirates were largely illiterate, few of their own words are to be found in the record that they left behind. Pirates have therefore been easy for more orthodox historians to ignore; few have dared, for example, to examine the unique role that black seamen and tradesmen played aboard pirate ships. The situation has also made it easy for novelists and filmmakers to impose their own imaginations on historical pirates and their secretive world.

This book is an introduction to the real world of the pirates. I hope that this firsthand view of objects that real pirates once owned and handled will help bring readers to a new realization of who these men really were, and to inspire some to undertake their own expeditions of discovery.

I would like to thank the National Geographic Society, Arts and Exhibitions International, and all of the men and women who have contributed to this project through the years.

It is to those men and women that this book is gratefully dedicated.

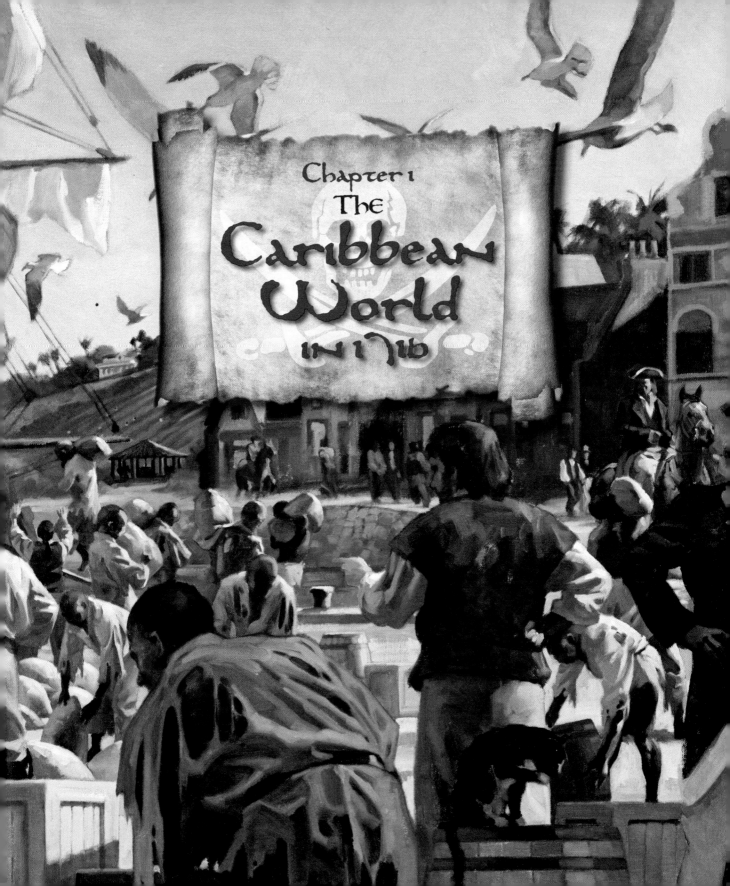

Chapter 1
The Caribbean World
in 1716

In 1716, the islands and coastlines encircling the Caribbean Sea represented a dynamic center of the Western world. With its enormous sugar plantations, and with vast quantities of South American gold and silver moving through its waters, the Caribbean world drew money, goods, and people from all corners of the Atlantic.

Much of the wealth of the Caribbean was built on the work of slaves. Their labor drove the region's plantation economy, and that economy established the wealth of the European empires that had built their colonies in the New World.

A few thousand pirates roamed its waters, determined to get a piece of the action.

The New World Economy

Over a period of 300 years and more, beginning around 1500, vast riches—billions of dollars in today's terms—flowed from the New World to Europe. England, France, Holland, Portugal, and Spain were the main players in this Atlantic economy. Their trade routes linked Europe, Africa, and the Americas.

A wide array of goods moved across and through the Atlantic Ocean in the early 18th century. Firearms, gunpowder, cloth, liquor, bar iron, pewterware, beads, and hand tools moved from Europe to Africa. Captives from Africa were transported in slave ships to the Caribbean and North and South America. Gold and ivory from Africa traveled in the same ships' holds back to Europe.

A trading boom drove an international traffic in goods—and people—between Europe, Africa, and America. Agricultural crops, such as cotton and sugar, were grown and processed in the Americas and shipped back to Europe. Plantation and natural products from the Caribbean and South America—primarily sugar, tobacco, and coffee—sailed back to Europe. Illegally traded provisions, especially

CARIBBEAN WATERFRONT

Preceding pages: At a time when the North American mainland was still largely an undeveloped frontier, the Caribbean was the economic power-house of the Atlantic world. Docks in the major port cities pulsated with trade and industry.

GVINEA propria, nec non NIGRITIÆ vel Terræ NIGRORVM maxima pars. La GVINEE de meme que la plus grande Partie du Pais des NEGRES, appellées Geographis hodiernis dicta utraq ÆTHIOPIA INFERIOR, & tujus quidem pars australis in delineationibus par les Geographes modernes ETHIOPIE INFERIEVRE & meridionale aures des morceaux geographiques Auxilliamus itineri Guineensi D. de Marchais ostensis secundum Leges projectionis stereographicæ Hassiana de Mr d'Anville, qui il a inseré au Voyage du Cheu de Marchais, & puis dessinée suivant designatæ & editæ studio & labore Homannianorum Heredum Norimb. cum Privil. S. C. M. A.1743 les Loix de la nouvelle projection de seu Mr le Prof. Has, par les Heritiers d'Homann A.1743

rum made from Caribbean sugar, moved from the North American colonies back to the Caribbean for sale.

Many Europeans were migrating to the Caribbean to share in the enormous fortunes generated by the sugar industry established there. Some were plantation owners and colonial administrators, living in positions of power and privilege.

WEST AFRICA, 1743

European slavers worked the West African coast north to south, from modern Gambia to Angola, and sold captives into slavery in the Caribbean.

All this wealth was transported across oceans that were barely policed. To pirates on the lookout for opportunity, it was all there for the taking.

A Slave-Based Economy

The entire system of Atlantic trade and Caribbean production depended on unpaid forced labor. Millions of Africans were either captured in war or kidnapped from their home territories, then shipped across the Atlantic.

Once they reached the Caribbean, they were sold in slave markets to plantation owners. As slaves, they had no rights. They were the property of the people who bought them. They spent their lives in backbreaking, sunup-to-sundown work.

Native Americans from the colonies of North and South America were also sold or kidnapped into slavery. With no previous exposure to tropical or European diseases, people like the Pequot of Connecticut had little resistance to sickness. Many died soon after reaching the Caribbean. For this reason, African slaves were more highly prized by the plantation owners.

Indentured servants came from Europe to work on the plantations. Some signed a contract binding them to work for a set period of years as a way to buy their passage to the New World. Others were convicts or political prisoners, sentenced to specific periods of forced labor. Many were Irish, kidnapped off the street and transported against their will. Indentured servants, like slaves, were owned by their masters, but only for the period specified in their contract. Their contracts could be extended without their knowledge or permission, however. Frequently, indentured servants were sold from one owner to another.

SILVER INGOTS

Indians, forced into labor, slaved in the mines of South America, loosening silver ore and carrying it on their backs out of the mines and up into the daylight. Then the ore was cast into discs, bars, or ingots. Much was converted into coins.

HENDRICK QUINTOR

Hendrick Quintor, a former sailor, was born in Amsterdam around 1692. Of African and Dutch descent, Quintor turned pirate when the Spanish brigantine he was on was captured.

Little is known about the lives of most black pirates. Piracy did offer black men an opportunity to participate on an equal footing, and some achieved leadership positions. Diego Grillo, a runaway slave from Havana, Cuba, commanded a ship in Captain Morgan's expedition against Panama. Francisco Farnando of Jamaica retired after a spectacular haul of 250,000 pieces of eight in a single robbery in 1715. Hendrick van der Heul served as quartermaster on the crew of the infamous Captain Kidd.

CARIBBEAN PLANTATIONS

Preceding pages: A huge workforce was necessary for the massive plantations of the Caribbean. The vast profits were created by the slave labor of millions, mostly Africans.

Men were forced into labor at sea as well as on land. Many sailors were press-ganged—kidnapped by gangs and pressed, or forced, to work on naval ships against their will. Some were abandoned without pay by unscrupulous merchant captains when they reached the New World, with no way to get home.

On land and at sea, the life of working people was hard. In 1713, the Treaty of Utrecht ushered in peace among the warring European powers. Navies were extensively demobilized, and large numbers of seamen were thrown out of work. Those who found employment experienced their poorest pay and working conditions for decades.

With so much wealth on the move, and so much discontent, conditions were ripe for piracy.

The Slave Ship Whydah

The first object which saluted my eyes when I arrived on the coast was the sea, and a slave-ship, which was then riding at anchor, and waiting for its cargo. These filled me with astonishment, which was soon converted into terror, which I am yet at a loss to describe, nor the then feelings of my mind.
—Olaudah Equiano, *The Interesting Narrative of the Life of Olaudah Equiano, or Gustavus Vassa the African*

The *Whydah Galley*—named for the slave port Ouidah (Wee-dah)—was built in London in 1715 as a slave ship. She left on her maiden voyage in early 1716. This 300-ton galley could be rowed or sailed. She represented the best nautical technology of her day. She was a shallow-drafted vessel with a low silhouette, easy to maneuver, and unusually fast, capable of speeds of up to 13 knots. Like all slave ships, the *Whydah* carried an arsenal of weaponry, which included 18 mounted cannon, for defense against attacks by Africans, European warships—or pirates.

On her maiden voyage, the *Whydah* set sail from London, out the English Channel and into the Atlantic, then turned south toward the African coast. Slave ships like the *Whydah* worked their way south and east around the West African coast from modern Gambia and Senegal to Nigeria and Gabon, filling their holds with slaves until they had a full load of "human cargo." Captives might be on board for months, waiting for the ship to fill, before they set sail to cross the Atlantic, Caribbean-bound.

AUCTION BLOCK

Soon after slaving ships reached the Caribbean, the captives on board were sold to plantation owners. People were placed on auction blocks and put up for sale, as if they were animals or farm equipment.

A WEST INDIAN MERCHANT SHIP
SAILING BETWEEN ENGLAND, AFRICA
AND THE ISLAND OF JAMAICA WITH
CARGOES OF SUGAR, RUM, SLAVES, GOLD
SILVER, IVORY AND TRADING GOODS.
SHE WAS SAID TO BE A VERY FINE
LONDON BUILT GALLEY OF 30 GUNS AND
"A SHIP OF ABOUT 300 TONS".
ON A RETURN TRIP TO ENGLAND SHE
WAS CAPTURED BY THE PIRATE

CAPT. SAMUEL "BLACK" BELLAMY
AND USED AS FLAGSHIP OF HIS FLEET.
SAILING NORTHWARD, CAPE COD
TRADITION TELLS US, TO CLAIM A
FAIR MAID OF WELLFLEET, HIS
SHIP WAS WRECKED APRIL 26, 1717
WITH THE LOSS OF NEAR 150 MEN.
HER BONES AND THE TREASURE
SHE CARRIED STILL LIE HIDDEN IN THE
SANDS OF THE GREAT BEACH.

WHIDAH

© STEVE POPE 1985

BUILT FOR THE TRADE

Slaving ships like the *Whydah* were custom-built for the slave trade. Over a span of almost 400 years, about 12 million Africans were transported to the Americas in such vessels.

The *Whydah* was an independent ship. Most of the English slave trade was controlled by the Royal African Company, which licensed many independents like the *Whydah*. The independent traders who owned a ship like the *Whydah* were originally known as "separate traders" or "ten percent men" because they paid ten percent of the value of the outbound cargo of each voyage to the Royal African Company. The remaining profits they divided among themselves.

The Slave Trade

The horrors I saw and felt cannot be well described; I saw many of my miserable countrymen chained two and two, some hand-cuffed, and some with their hands tied behind.

—Ottobah Cugoano, *Thoughts and Sentiments on the Evil and Wicked Traffic of the Slavery and Commerce of the Human Species*

The English and other Europeans formed lucrative alliances with local African leaders. They built and ran a series of forts that dotted the African coast. All told, 12 million Africans are believed to have been transported to the Americas. Fully half of them were shipped between 1700 and 1807 or 1808, the years of the abolition of the slave trade in Britain and the United States, respectively. Half of this number (about 3.5 million) were delivered by U.S. and British ships.

Captives were brought to these forts by African merchants and crammed into windowless, airless, unsanitary dungeons called truncks or barracoons. Eventually the imprisoned captives were sold to representatives from the European companies. Their journey to the Caribbean was about to begin.

Captives were sold in bulk, not as individuals. A document from 1731 records the exchange of 40 captives in Ouidah. They were sold to the Royal African Company for:

- 337 trading guns
- 40 muskets
- 530 pounds of gunpowder.

Since the *Whydah* was an independent trader, captives were probably bought and brought on board in twos and threes, not in large groups, as would have been the case on ships operated by the Royal African Company.

THE ATLANTIC WORLD, 1719

Following pages: In the early 1700s, the wealth of the Caribbean was established, its riches transported back to Europe. North America was still a frontier. Some cities in the Spanish Main were much bigger than the tiny North American cities. Goods and people moved up and down the Atlantic coast as if on a highway.

A New & Correct MAP of the WHOLE WORLD

THE ICE SEA

THE NORTH

THE RUSSE SEA

NOVA ZEMBLA

MARE GLACIALE

Artick Circle

EASTERN

OCEAN or

Parts Unknown

SAMOIDA

TONGUSIEN

The Plain of BARGU

LAPLAND

RUSSIA

GREAT TARTARY

EASTERN or

CHINESIAN-

Dominions of the Czar of Russia or Moscovy

SIBIRIA

EUROPE

POLAND

TARTARY

LAND OF IESSO

Company's Land

ASTRACAN

KALMUCKS LAND

CIRCASSIAN TARTARY

BLACK SEA

CASPIAN SEA

INDEPENDENT TARTARY

USBECK

CASGAR

MONGULS

SEA OF CORFA

IAPON

BULGISTAN

PERSIA

TIBET

CHINA

ARABIA

MOGUL

INDIA

AFRICA

NEGROLAND

BENGALA

INDIAN SEA

Ladrone Islands

GUINEA

ETHIOPIA

Equinoctial Line

CEYLON

THE EASTERN or

SUNDA ISLANDS

BORNEO

ETHIOPIAN

MONOEMUGI

INDIAN OCEAN

CARPENTARIA

Dimens Land

MONOMOTAPA

Tropick of Capricorn

NEW HOLLAND

Kendracht Land

SEA

Cape of Good Hope

Nuyts Land

Lewins Land

Variable Winds

OCEAN

A SCALE of English Leagues.

EXPLANATION

A New & Correct MAP of the WHOLE WORLD Shewing ye Situation of its Principal Parts. Viz the Seas, Kingdoms, Rivers, Capes, Ports, Mountains, Woods, Trade-Winds, Monsoons, Variation of ye Compass, Climats, &c.

The Projection of this Map is Call'd Mercator's, the Designe is to make it Useful both for Land and Sea. And it is laid Down with all possible Care, according to ye Newest & Most Exact Observations

By HERMAN MOLL Geographer. 1719.

Sold by H. Moll where you may have his New Atlas or Sett of Twenty Seven Two-sheet Maps, bound or single, all Colour'd according to his Directions, over against Deveroux Court, between Temple Bar and St Clement's Church, in the Strand.

Sold by I. King at the Globe in the Poultrey near Stocks Market.

A scale model of the *Whydah* shows parts of the deck, including the bell, wheel, and rigging, as they may have looked. This reconstruction is based on the best information available for similar ships of the period.

The Xwéda Kingdom, in the region of modern-day Benin, was wealthy and densely populated in the early 18th century. With the coming of Europeans and their slave-trade economy, the small coastal village of Ouidah evolved into one of the most important centers of the West African slave trade. The city neared the height of its prosperity between 1700 and 1720.

The kings of Xwéda and the neighboring kingdom of Dahomey were active participants in the transatlantic slave trade. They collected a tax from the Europeans for each captive loaded onto a slave ship. Every year, between 15,000 and 20,000 captive people left the town of Ouidah against their will, bound for slave markets in the New World.

Like Caribbean towns on the other side of the Atlantic, Ouidah attracted a motley group of people. It was a free port, so ships from any European nation could anchor in its harbor. The French, British, and Portuguese all maintained forts in Ouidah and provided work for many Africans from the Gold Coast.

The people sold to European traders in Ouidah were not from Ouidah itself. They were captured inland, one hundred or more miles away. They came from many ethnic groups and spoke many languages. Some were from farming communities, others from towns.

Most of the captives were prisoners of war, victims of local conflicts. With so much money riding on the trade, enslaving enemies became an excuse for war. Those taken into captivity were terrorized, grief-stricken, and confused. African merchants marched them along trade routes to the coast, where they sold them to Europeans.

The price paid for a slave depended on his or her physical health. Ship's doctors inspected and sorted the captives. They were branded, like cattle, with the ship's name.

European slave buyers in the Caribbean wanted young people—they were stronger and healthier, with more years of work to come. So the majority of

PREPARING FOR PASSAGE

Captives were brought from inland Africa to slaving ports on the west coast. When they arrived there, they were inspected by ship's doctors before being brought aboard. European slavers only bought Africans they considered healthy.

BELOW DECKS

Ships slowly filled up with captives. Most waited on board for months before they left the African coast. The average time on the ship was eight months, but some were on board for as long as eighteen.

captives taken were 16 to 30 years old. One in seven was a child, only 10 to 15 years old. Roughly two out of three were males. Girls and women were valued more greatly by the Africans, since they were needed locally to work in the fields and produce more children. For these reasons, female captives could cost twice as much as their male counterparts.

The coast at Ouidah was low-lying. Captives were ferried out through heavy surf to the large slave ships that anchored more than a mile off the coast. Despite their restraints, many of those captured chose to throw themselves overboard before they even reached the ships.

Resistance to the Slave Trade

Europeans built forts and patrolled the African coast for good reason. Africans frequently attacked Europeans and their ships, trying to rescue people destined for the slave trade. Although the captives were heavily guarded and shackled, revolt and mutiny were regular occurrences on board the ships as well.

In 1807 the British Parliament passed the Abolition of the Slave Trade Act, outlawing any engagement in the slave trade throughout the British colonies. The United States passed a similar law in 1808.

But illegal trafficking continued, and slavery itself was not abolished. It wasn't until the end of the Civil War in 1865 that slavery was declared unconstitutional throughout the United States.

In 1839 a group of Africans sold into slavery took over a Spanish slave ship, the *Amistad,* off the coast of Cuba. They demanded to be taken back to Africa. The crew tricked them, and sailed the vessel instead up the North American coast. The ship was intercepted by the U.S. Coast Guard off Long Island, New York, near Culloden Point.

At their trial in New Haven, Connecticut, John Quincy Adams—no longer U. S. President but by then a congressman from Massachusetts—represented the Africans who had taken over the *Amistad.* They received significant support from abolitionists as well. In 1841, the *Amistad* slaves won their freedom when the U.S. Supreme Court proclaimed their enslavement illegal. They raised money by giving public lectures and finally returned to Africa in 1842.

SHACKLES

Male captives were shackled together in pairs to prevent rebellion and suicides. Many West Africans believed that if they died in their native land, their spirits would remain close to friends and families.

The Middle Passage

By the time the *Whydah* left Ouidah, more than 300 captives, destined to be sold into slavery in the Caribbean, had been crammed into her hold. The ship embarked on the long transatlantic journey called the "Middle Passage," a term referring to the slaving voyage between the African coast and Caribbean slave markets. The Atlantic crossing was the middle leg of the slaving trade route: Europe to Africa, Africa to the Americas, and America back to Europe.

To maximize profits, ships were often overloaded. Captives were held in hot, foul spaces so small they could only crouch or lie down. If there was room for 400 captives, 550 or 600 might be packed in. Wooden tubs were used as latrines. The air was sometimes so bad that there wasn't enough oxygen for a candle to burn.

A barricade divided the ship in half, separating the men from the women and children. Men, women, and children were allowed on deck during the daytime in good weather. The men were restrained; the women and children were not.

On board, captives were forced to exercise by dancing on the deck when the weather allowed it. Those who refused were beaten by members of the ship's crew. Armed guards prevented mutinies.

An average Atlantic crossing took eight to twelve weeks. In poor weather conditions, it could last more than ten. Many Africans died during the voyage, some from disease, others from a poor diet, lack of food, or inadequate care.

Diseases like dysentery, smallpox, measles, and scurvy spread without mercy. If captives died, their bodies were thrown overboard without burial rites or ceremony. Many went on hunger strikes. Whole ships sometimes participated. Anyone who refused food was force-fed.

Special netting was installed on deck to prevent suicide—the only possible escape. The captain and crew on slave ships armed themselves for the worst. Dust

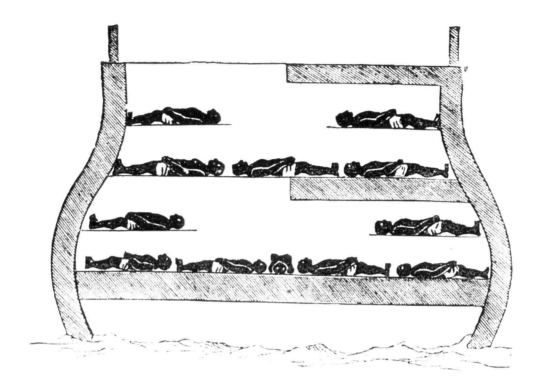

Coupe de face d'un navire négrier, capturé en 1843.

shot—tiny lead riot-control pellets that were useless in actual battle—has been found only at slave ship wreck sites. Peppering rioting captives with dust shot avoided permanent damage to the valuable human cargo.

Firsthand Knowledge

CROSS SECTION OF A SLAVE SHIP'S HOLD

Captives were held in darkness on platforms with headroom only two and a half feet high. They were forced to remain in such spaces for 16 to 20 hours a day, not even able to sit up.

Olaudah Equiano, a former slave, published his autobiography, *The Interesting Narrative of the Life of Olaudah Equiano, or Gustavus Vassa the African*, in England in 1789. Most historians believe that Equiano was born in

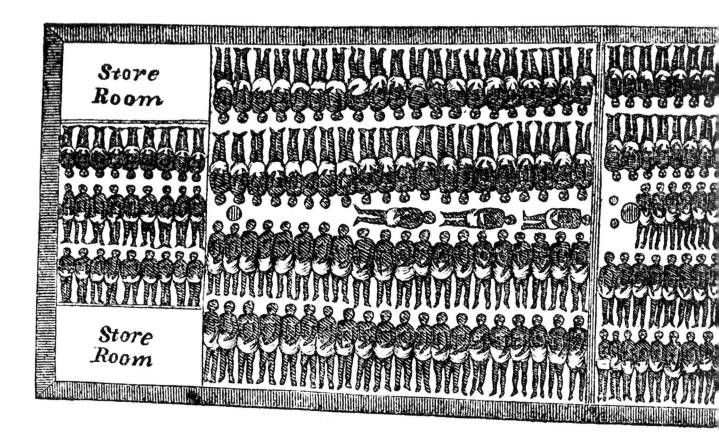

Store Room

Store Room

SLAVES IN HOLD

Captives were lined up like merchandise inside the slave ships. Constantly under guard, they resisted in many ways, and often. They jumped overboard to their death, went on hunger strikes, and participated in revolts, attempting to take over the ship.

Africa, though some claim that he was born in the Americas. But none doubt the accuracy of his description of the slave trade.

Equiano's book was the earliest firsthand account of the slave trade by an ex-slave. It became an immediate bestseller. It contributed to the abolition of the slave trade in England in 1807 and inspired Frederick Douglass to write his own autobiography.

Here are two extracts from Equiano's book that describe the Middle Passage:

The stench of the hold while we were on the coast was so intolerably loathsome that it was dangerous to remain there for any time, and some of us had been

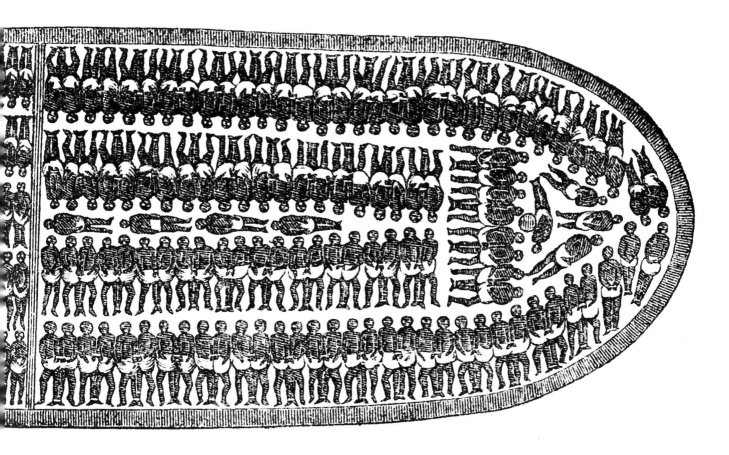

permitted to stay on the deck for the fresh air; but now that the whole ship's cargo were confined together, it became absolutely pestilential. The closeness of the place, and the heat of the climate, added to the number in the ship, which was so crowded that each had scarcely room to turn himself, almost suffocated us.

This wretched situation was again aggravated by the galling of the chains, now become insupportable; and the filth of the necessary tubs, into which the children often fell, and were almost suffocated. The shrieks of the women, and the groans of the dying, rendered the whole a scene of horror almost inconceivable.

Akan Gold

Some of the finest treasure found in the wreckage of the *Whydah* was Akan gold jewelry. This gold was traded in Africa and carried in slave ships to Europe, where it was melted down and recast.

The Akan live in parts of modern Ghana and southeastern Ivory Coast. They include several groups, including the Asante and Fante of Ghana and the Baule and Agni peoples of the Ivory Coast. They have mined, worked, and traded gold for centuries. On European maps of the 18th century, their region was called the "Gold Coast."

The Akan cast gold and developed weighing systems. They traded with North African Islamic merchants who crossed the Sahara Desert in camel caravans and accepted Akan gold in exchange for salt, textiles, leather, weapons, and brassware.

Europeans bought Akan jewelry from the North African traders. In the late 1400s, the Portuguese decided to cut out the North African middlemen and went to the West African coast to trade directly with the Akan. Soon they started to trade with other Africans, buying humans and transporting them across the Atlantic. Along with gold dust and nuggets, Akan gold jewelry was used as currency in the trade. Experts have identified these artifacts as the world's oldest reliably dated examples of Akan jewelry.

AFRICAN TREASURE

When first discovered in the *Whydah* shipwreck, pieces of Akan gold often peeked out from unassuming concretions, above.

Opposite: One small, high-karat gold bead found in the wreckage *(far left)* was probably from a necklace, bracelet, or anklet.

Akan royals of both sexes wore necklaces, bracelets, and knee or elbow decorations. Others wore jewelry made of gold money,

like the reconstructed Akan money necklace *(second from left)*. The rectangular bead *(second from right)* was one of the largest

types of beads produced by Akan goldsmiths, worn by a king or chief at special ceremonies but kept hidden under his clothes.

Akan goldsmiths often made jewelry in the shape of bells, such as the cast-gold pendant *(far right),* which might have been part of

a bracelet or necklace.

WRITTEN FROM EXPERIENCE

As a firsthand account of the experience of a slave, Olaudah Equiano's 1789 *Narrative* was one of the great exceptions. Millions of people's stories were lost forever. Twelve million African people made the treacherous passage to the Americas, yet only 15 firsthand accounts of the journey survive.

Olaudah Equiano,

OR

GUSTAVUS VASSA,

the African.

Publish'd March 1. 1789 by G. Vassa.

The Whydah Completes her Maiden Slaving Voyage

When a ship carrying its human cargo across the Atlantic from Africa finally reached its Caribbean destination, the captives were given medical attention and briefly allowed to recuperate. As soon as they were considered "refreshed"—recovered enough to be put on sale—they were auctioned off in slave markets. Equiano wrote of such an experience firsthand:

> We were not many days in the merchant's custody, before we were sold after their usual manner, which is this: On a signal given, (as the beat of a drum) the buyers rush at once into the yard where the slaves are confined, and make choice of that parcel they like best. The noise and clamor with which this is attended, and the eagerness visible in the countenances of the buyers, serve not a little to increase the apprehension of terrified Africans, ...
>
> In this manner, without scruple, are relations and friends separated, most of them never to see each other again.

Those captives who survived the Whydah's voyage were sold in the slave markets.

Emptied of her human cargo but flush with the profits of her trade, the Whydah made her way back out through the Caribbean, very likely proceeding through the Windward Passage—the current-swept waters between Cuba and Hispaniola—with stops along the way as the ship prepared to cross the Atlantic on her return trip to England.

PHYSICIAN'S SYRINGES

Early 18th-century surgeons used syringes to inject mercury compounds directly into ailing body parts to balance the humors, or essential bodily fluids.

Chapter 2
Capturing The Whydah

amuel Bellamy was born on March 18, 1689, into a poor family near Plymouth, Devon, England. His mother died at or soon after his birth, and Sam had to start working at a young age. Considering the skill he later showed as a ship's captain, he may well have spent some of his early years in the Royal Navy or as a privateer.

The historical record does not provide firm information, but it does indicate that Sam Bellamy traveled from England to the New World by 1714.

At the age of 24, Bellamy—now unemployed—sailed to the colonies to seek his fortune. Legend has it that he stayed with relatives in Wellfleet, Massachusetts, where he saw a beautiful young woman, "a yellow-haired girl with eyes like the sea," sitting under an apple tree, surrounded by a mist of white blossoms. According to the story, Bellamy fell instantly in love. The young woman, Maria Hallett, came from a family of prosperous farmers. They wouldn't consider allowing their daughter to marry a penniless, out-of-work sailor.

When word reached Cape Cod that a Spanish treasure fleet had been wrecked off the coast of Florida, Bellamy saw his opportunity to get rich and impress Maria's family. Through his uncle he had met Palgrave Williams, a local goldsmith, who loaned him enough money to buy a ship and hire a crew.

Despite being a respectable, settled, 39-year-old tradesman, Williams threw in his hat and came aboard with Bellamy. The two set off for a treasure-seeking adventure. Purportedly promising Maria that he would make a fortune and return soon to Massachusetts, Bellamy set sail for Florida.

The news of a sunken treasure off Florida was not simply a rumor. On July 31, 1715, the Spanish treasure fleet had set sail for Spain from Havana, Cuba. The ships were crammed with gold and silver from mines deep in the mountains of Mexico, Peru, and Bolivia. Without warning, a massive hurricane struck the fleet. Helpless against the storm, a thousand men drowned, and the Crown's treasure ended up at the bottom of the sea.

PIRATE ATTACK

Preceding pages: Sam Bellamy and his crew had taken dozens of ships in the Caribbean before they captured the *Whydah.* For example, they boarded the *Sainte Marie,* a French frigate, off the northwest coast of Cuba.

As soon as the word spread, fortune hunters—including Sam Bellamy—headed down to Florida. The Spanish royal court acted quickly to protect their valuable cargo, however. The fleet had sunk in shallow waters, and the Spaniards safely recovered much of their riches.

Looking to get in on the action, the governor of Jamaica issued privateering commissions that authorized robbing enemy ships.

But London had made peace with Spain, and the British government quickly declared the privateers illegal. Their activities no longer sanctioned by the state, the privateers were now outlaws.

They had become pirates.

Who Were the Pirates?

I am a free Prince, and I have as much authority to make war on the whole world as he who has a hundred sail of ships at sea, and an army of 100,000 men in the Field, and this my conscience tells me.

—Sam Bellamy

As long as people and goods have moved on water, there have been pirates. By definition, pirates rob ships at sea. Several different sorts of seafaring brigands plied the waves through the years. Here are some forerunners of the pirates of the early 18th century.

- Privateers were legal pirates. A commission or license—sometimes called a "letter of marque"—granted a privateer permission to attack and rob the ships of enemy nations. In return, privateers shared their takings with the authorities. They were a cheap way for states to attack their enemies and minimize the expense of running a navy during wartime. And the king got a cut of his privateers' takings. But once the war ended, it wasn't always easy to control the privateers. By the early 18th century most of the European states had signed peace treaties with each other. No longer at war, they stopped issuing privateer licenses.

- Corsairs were pirates who operated out of Mediterranean ports from the time of the Crusades until the early 1800s.

- Buccaneers were pirates active in the Caribbean during the 1600s. Mostly French, but also English and Dutch, they were famous for their daring and

KNUCKLE GUARD

This plain, wood-handled, double-shell knuckle guard belonged to a cutlass. Short, thick, and wide, cutlasses usually attached to a pirate's wrist with a cord.

SAM BELLAMY

Sam Bellamy, commanding officer of the *Whydah,* came from a background typical of many an early 18th-century pirate. An experienced sailor from a poor family, he had little to lose by "going on the account."

Sam Bellamy became one of the most successful pirate captains of his day, quickly acquiring a small flotilla and looting dozens of ships in a year-long voyage that took him through the Caribbean and back up the North American coast. When the *Whydah* sank, she was packed with large quantities of gold and silver, testimony to Sam Bellamy's success as a looter and leader of a pirate crew.

violent raids on Spanish ships and cities. Before becoming pirates, many lived as hunters who formed their own outlaw communities in the woods of Hispaniola, the island now made up of Haiti and the Dominican Republic. The name "buccaneer" comes from the French word *boucan*, the place where the men cured and smoked strips of meat.

THE ISLAND OF TORTUGA

Named for its turtle shape, Tortuga is a small island off the north coast of Haiti. It became home to the buccaneers around 1630. Its location between the islands of Hispaniola and Cuba made it a favored refuge for sea brigands.

Most of those who became pirates were already experienced sailors. In the early 1700s, life on board navy and merchant ships was grim. The work was punishing, the hours were long, discipline was severe, beatings were

common, the hierarchy was strict, food was inadequate, disease was rife, and the pay was bad … if you got paid at all.

Life on a pirate ship was a very different experience. The men elected their own officers, decided on their ship's course and operations, and got equal shares in the booty. Crews were large, so the work was a lot lighter. Discipline was lax and rum was plentiful.

In times of war, sailors could easily gain employment on merchant or navy vessels. But during peacetime and periods of high unemployment, many seamen, given the chance, opted for the pirate's life.

Pirates of previous generations had attacked the ships of enemy nations, but in the early 1700s, known as the "Golden Age of Piracy," they swore loyalty to no nation. Opportunists, they attacked all shipping equally, turning themselves into enemies of any and all nations. The penalty for piracy was death by hanging. Once a man made the decision to "go on the account" and join a pirate crew, he had nothing—and everything—to lose.

Pirates mostly lived on board ship and stayed on the move to avoid capture. They might spend the summer in an out-of-the-way location like Newfoundland or Madagascar, however, fixing up their ships in preparation for a season spent plundering the Caribbean or the Red Sea.

Dotted around the maritime world were places that pirates used as bases of operations, safe harbors where a pirate ship could dock or anchor without fear of attack or capture. Once ashore, the crew could fence their goods, repair their ships, and spend their loot on wine, women, and song.

What made for a good pirate refuge?

- It was far away from regularly patrolled waters yet still close to lucrative shipping lanes.
- The local authorities turned a blind eye to activities going on in nearby waters.

Some authorities actually found it to their advantage to allow piracy in their jurisdictions. With their heavily armed ships and reckless reputations, pirates could offer protection against political enemies.

- Finally, it had to be a place where the local economy flourished. Pirates were looking for a place where they could sell their loot, spend their money, and stock up on supplies like provisions and rigging.

During the early 1700s, certain places came to be known as favored by pirates. These places made up part of the so-called pirate round:

Sallée, on the Atlantic coast of Morocco, was one of the legendary corsair towns, an infamous stopping-place for pirates between 1000 and 1700.

Tripoli, a coastal town in modern Libya, was also favored by the corsairs from 1000 to 1800.

Called Leghorn by Englishmen in the 1600s, Livorno, Italy, where the Arno River empties into the Adriatic Sea, was a pirate haven.

Nice, in southern France, and Livorno served as bases for 17th-century English pirates who attacked ships on the Mediterranean.

Roaringwater Bay, between Cape Clear and Mizen Head on the southwest coast of Ireland, was a favorite hiding place for Irish and English pirates in the 1600s.

The island of Newfoundland, Canada, provided an isolated, and cool, safe haven in the summer for pirates.

Madagascar, east of southern Africa in the Indian Ocean, was a famed residence for European and Caribbean pirates from the 1690s through the 1730s.

Port Royal, Jamaica, was a central stopover on the Caribbean trade routes and a famous haunt for buccaneers and pirates until the city was destroyed by an earthquake and tsunami in 1692.

BAR SHOT

Bar shot, one of the many types of shot recovered from the *Whydah,* sped out of a cannon and tumbled on impact. When fired into the rigging of a retreating ship, bar shot shredded sails and slowed down a vessel so that pirates could catch up and board.

New Providence, Bahamas, the island dominated today by the city of Nassau, was called a "nest of pirates" and became the new headquarters for pirates after the destruction of Port Royal.

Tortuga, an island off the coast of modern-day Haiti, was the base of operations for buccaneers, far from the reach of the authorities.

BOARDING AT SEA

Pirate crews were so large and well armed, they could overwhelm a passing merchant ship, as shown in this painting by Frederick Judd Waugh.

VIEW OF PORT ROYAL, 1758

Preceding pages: Merchant vessels hoist sail near Port Royal, Jamaica, the natural harbor shown to the left in this painting. A pirate lair until it was leveled by an earthquake in 1692, it rose again and the rebuilt harbor became a major port of commerce in the 18th century. Morant Bay Fort, in the foreground, was built in 1758.

On the Account

If men are denied the chance to live in freedom, they will make their own freedom.

—written on the wall of a 17th-century tavern, as quoted by Frank Sherry, *Raiders and Rebels*

By the time Bellamy reached Florida, representatives of the Spanish crown had hired local Indian divers to retrieve the sunken treasure. They stored what they could find in a fort onshore. Learning of this, English privateer Henry Jennings raided the Spanish fort. He and his crew escaped with well over 120,000 pieces of eight. This outlandish act of independent thievery launched a new era of piracy.

It was all too tempting for Sam Bellamy. One way or the other, he was determined to make his fortune. He decided to go on the account—to commit himself to the life of a pirate. The rest of the crew agreed. Their travels and confrontations have been put together from court records and eyewitness accounts.

February 1716: Gulf of Honduras

Leaving Florida, Bellamy and his crew sailed south to the Gulf of Honduras.

March 1716: Portobello, Panama

Working their way toward the southwest along the Central American coast, they staged a raid at or near Portobello, Panama, a major port in the Caribbean trade economy.

April 1716: Baya Honda, Cuba

Sailing north through the Caribbean, Bellamy joined forces with Henry Jennings,

HOUSEHOLD ITEMS

The octagonal base of a pewter candlestick *(opposite)* represents a rare Jacobean style from the 1660s to 1680s. The Queen Anne-style pewter teapot *(below)* would be charming were it not that a leg bone was found jammed in its ebony handle in the *Whydah* wreckage.

Grenades, although they caused little damage, helped disorganize resistance. Here one sits in a freshwater conservation bath. With the exception of the wreck of a British troopship located in Canadian waters, more grenades have been recovered from the *Whydah* site than from any other 18th-century shipwreck.

the English pirate. On the northwest coast of Cuba, near today's district of Pinar del Rio, they spotted a French frigate, the *Sainte Marie,* and decided to seize her. They struck in *periaguas*—large dugout canoes. The surprised crew of the *Sainte Marie* fought back, but the pirates took their ship, along with 30,000 pieces of eight—the currency of the Caribbean at the time.

Late April 1716: Cape Corrientes and the Isle of Pines, Cuba

Before long, Bellamy split from Jennings to join Capt. Ben Hornigold's pirate flotilla. They captured a French sloop, the *Marianne.* Hornigold gave the ship to Bellamy, whose crew included at this point Palgrave Williams and Richard Caverley out of Rhode Island, Swedish-born Peter Cornelius Hoof,

a Dutch mulatto known as Hendrick Quintor, John Fletcher and Jeremiah Higgins from a prize vessel called the *Blackett*, and dozens of other marauders from all corners of the Atlantic. Sailing east and then south around the island of Cuba, the pirates robbed ships off Cape Corrientes and the Isle of Pines, today's Isla de la Juventud.

May 1716: Eastern tip of Cuba

Heading eastward along the south shore of Cuba, Hornigold and Bellamy reached the far eastern tip of the island. Here they met up with a French pirate, a master of many aliases, perhaps christened as Olivier Le Vasseur but known to all as "La Buse—the Buzzard."

June to August 1716: North coast of Haiti

The pirate flotilla stopped to refit along the north coast of Hispaniola. Hornigold refused to attack any English ships, but Bellamy—who felt no loyalty toward any country and considered ships of all nations fair game—decided to challenge Hornigold's authority.

The dispute was put to a vote. The crew elected Bellamy captain. Hornigold left, accompanied by his supporters, including a sailor known as Edward Teach—who would soon become the legendary Blackbeard. Many of Hornigold's men elected to stay with Bellamy, however, including John Brown from Jamaica and Richard Noland from Ireland. Together with their followers, Bellamy and La Buse continued eastward.

September 1716: Puerto Rico

Bellamy, sailing the *Marianne*, reached the coast of Puerto Rico, where he attacked a 44-gun French ship. After an hour-long fight, he was driven off with little loss.

GRENADES

Boarders pelted the decks of a hostile ship with hand grenades before leaping over her side. Lines with heavy grappling hooks were tossed onto the enemy ship as well. Once such a grapnel had anchored itself, pirates could haul on the lines and draw the vessel nearer.

MAP OF THE ANTILLES, 1686

Following pages: Even before 1700, the many islands of the Caribbean had been charted and named, as documented in this French map of the region.

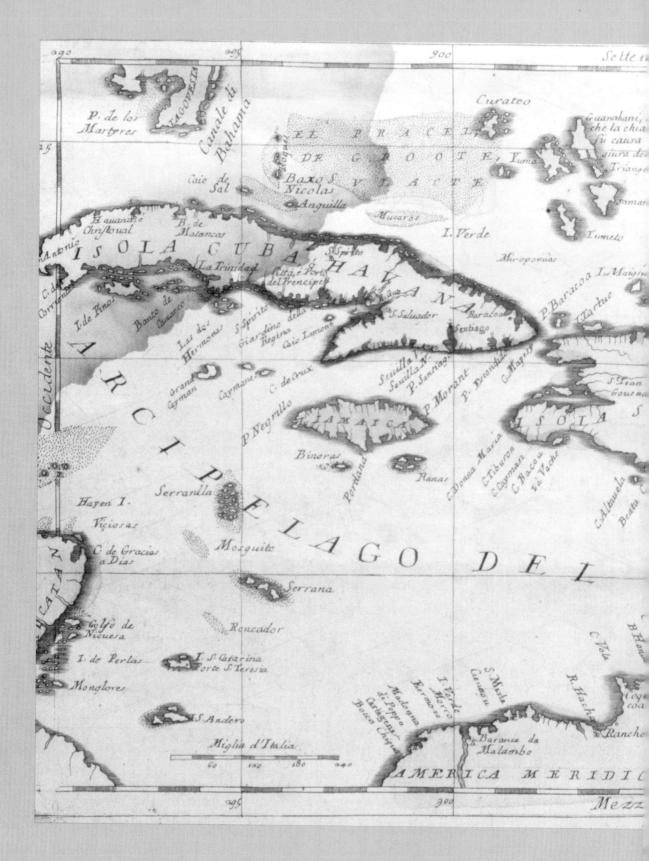

SILVER KNUCKLE GUARD

Part of a small sword, this knuckle guard would be used by an attacker to pull the blade of his own weapon from an opponent's chest after a deadly strike.

October 1716: Samana Bay to Cape Nicholas, Hispaniola

Turning back toward Haiti, Bellamy and La Buse attacked shipping all along the north coast of Hispaniola. La Buse took Simon van Vorst of New York and Thomas Baker, a Dutch tailor, from a ship off Cape Nicholas, on the northwest coast of Haiti. Baker later claimed that if he had refused to join the pirates, he would have been marooned.

November to December 1716: St. Croix

Sailing east, Bellamy and La Buse made their base on St. Croix for a few weeks. From there, they took at least a dozen ships in the Virgin and the Leeward Islands. They captured a prize, a galley called the *Sultana*, and converted her to a pirate ship. The pirates, who included the Scottish ship's surgeon, James Ferguson; an ex-privateer, Edward Moon; a veteran pirate, Joseph Rivers; and the gunner's mate, William Osborne—elected Sam Bellamy commander of their small fleet.

Bellamy made Palgrave Williams captain of the *Marianne*. Welshman Thomas Davis, a shipwright and carpenter aboard the captured *St. Michael*, and Boston-born Thomas South were forced to join the pirates. When the *Bonetta* was captured in November, there was a young boy aboard named John King, traveling from Jamaica to Antigua with his mother. King—perhaps as young as eight years old—was so enamored of the pirates and their life that he begged Bellamy to let him join the crew despite his mother's protests. Bellamy agreed, and the young boy became a pirate.

January 1717: La Isla Blanquilla, Venezuela

The flotilla headed south through the Caribbean toward Venezuela. On reaching the island of Blanquilla, just north of Margarita, La Buse chose to go his own way. After refitting at Los Testigos, a little farther to the west, Bellamy and Williams returned to St. Croix, where they rescued some French pirates whose ship had been sunk by a British Royal Navy vessel. These men were added to their crew. French gunner Jean Taffier also joined up.

Pirate Ships

Pirates may have taken their first vessel in a mutiny. Or they may have used canoes or rowboats to capture their first ship. Ships seized by force were called prizes.

Pirates used a variety of vessels: sloops, pinks, snows, galleys, and ships. Many pirate sloops were single-masted, fast, with up to 12 guns, and often fitted with oars. Two or three sloops would sail in consorts, forming a small flotilla.

Captain Kidd, Bart Roberts, and Blackbeard—all three of these notorious pirates had larger, three-masted warships:

- Blackbeard's *Queen Anne's Revenge* carried 40 guns;
- Kidd's *Adventure Galley,* designed as a privateer vessel, had 34 guns; and
- Roberts's *Royal Fortune* had 42 mounted guns.

Smaller consorts traveled with these ships. They served a key purpose: They could chase prey in shallow waters, where deeper-draft boats would run aground.

ACTION OFF CARTAGENA, 1708

Following pages: Representing a spectacular sea siege off the coast of Colombia, this painting by Samuel Scott shows a British privateer attacking ships near Cartagena, the port from which the Spanish treasure fleet sailed for Europe.

SWORD HILT

Grasping this hilt, a pirate could wield a poniard or a *main gauche* (left hand) weapon, used either as a long punch dagger or as the secondary weapon in a two-handed parry.

What is a sloop?

A sloop is a vessel with a single mast, a large fore-and-aft mainsail behind the mast, and one or two more jibs in front. Sloops generally carried a single square sail as well.

What is a pink?

A pink is a vessel of any size with a narrow, overhanging stern.

What is a snow?

A snow is the largest of all two-masted, squared-rigged vessels. A snow has a small mast, located just behind the main mast, which carries a large fore-and-aft sail called a trysail.

What is a galley?

A galley is a ship built for speed and maneuverability. A galley can move easily under the power of sweeps, or long oars, but it can also hoist sails in order to use the power of the wind.

What is a ship?

The term "ship" was reserved for the largest of all vessel types, a sailing boat with three or more masts, square-rigged sails on every one of them.

What is a ship's rigging?

Sailing ships of the 18th century had two types of rigging: standing and running. The standing rigging consisted of all the ropes that supported the masts. Deadeyes and lanyards were used to tighten the standing rigging.

Running rigging referred to all the equipment used to raise, lower, and trim the sails. It included blocks and tackle—a pulley or a set of pulleys with rope rove through to be used for hoisting—and halyards, the lines used to hoist and lower the sails.

CONCRETION

Articles lost for centuries in the briny deep off Cape Cod have been glued together into concretions, timebound collages of artifacts, stones, and sand. A strand of rope and a pistol mingle in this chunk.

How to Fire a Cannon

Cannon were kept loaded at all times on pirate ships.

1. First the crew hauled the gun in and secured it firmly using a preventer tackle.

2. Then they swabbed the muzzle out with a sponge and added a cartridge of gunpowder, packing it tightly into the chamber.

3. The cannonball—or shot—was rolled down the muzzle on top of the gunpowder.

4. The men stuffed cloth wadding on top of the shot to stop it rolling back out.

5. One man stuck a sharp-pointed quill or metal pick down the vent, to pierce the paper gunpowder cartridge, and poured in the priming powder.

6. As they moved the gun into position, ready to be fired, the crew slackened the preventer tackle and manned the side-tackles.

7. One of them laid a sheepskin over the touch hole at the rear of the cannon, then put a lead apron over it.

8. The gun crew carefully aimed the cannon at the target, following the directions of the gun captain.

9. They used a wedge-shaped quoin to adjust the angle of the gun.

10. As the ship caught a downward-rolling wave, the gun captain gave the order to fire. The rest of the gun crew stepped back while one seaman lit the powder in the vent with a hemp match. The flame moved along the powder train and lit the powder cartridge. The gun fired as the ship rolled back up to the crest of the wave. When it fired, the gun would recoil, or suddenly and quickly shoot backward. Anyone who got in the way could easily be knocked over and killed.

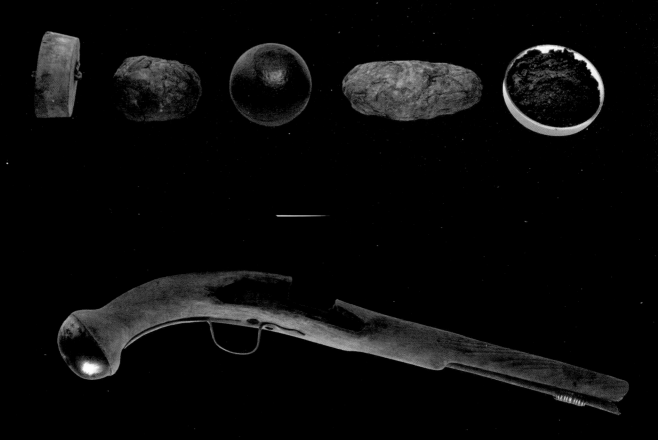

Pirate Boarding Parties

You're on the ocean, miles from land. A ship flying the Jolly Roger appears and fires a single warning shot. What would you do? Probably the same thing most crews did in the early 1700s: Surrender at once and avoid violence.

Pirates were well armed, ready to attack, with crews four or five times larger than that of a merchant ship. They were more interested in loot than in fighting. The goal of a boarding party was to terrorize the opponents—to scare them into cooperating as quickly as possible. If the pirates wanted the ship as a prize, they wouldn't blast its hull with cannonballs.

If they didn't want the ship, they might burn it after plundering it. If pirates wanted to rob a ship—especially if they also planned to convert it to their own use—they had no interest in causing damage. But if an intended victim put up resistance, the pirates struck without hesitation or mercy.

Pirates in the boarding party were armed with pikes—long spears with double-edged blades about four inches long, in the shape of a spike or a leaf. Other pikemen stood by on deck to fend off potential enemy boarders.

Pirates would lob grenades at their opponents as they boarded their ships. Loaded with gunpowder and ignited by a cloth fuse threaded through a wooden plug, the grenade would explode, causing confusion and terror. It could travel about 25 yards if thrown but even farther if fired from a small mortar called a cohorn.

Some grenades were used as incendiary devices. Flames would fan out from vents around the fuse plug, setting fire to the ship. Other grenades, loaded with compounds that caused potentially deadly fumes, were used to smoke out opponents. One recorded compound contained pitch, saltpeter, tar, sulfur, coal dust, asafetida, mercury, and ground-up animal hooves.

PIRATE WEAPONRY

Tampion (or gun-barrel cork), tamping materials, and gunpowder dust accompanied the spherical shot itself inside the gun barrel of a well-prepared pirate. A dated brass plate from a pistol *(lower left)* serves as an emblem of how weapons recovered from the *Whydah* by and large represented first-class, cutting-edge weapons technology.

SUN KING PISTOL

Although decorating the handle of a gun named for the Sun King—the moniker for France's Louis XIV—this grinning Celtic deity *(above)* claims the pistol for Britannia. In a case of royal one-upmanship, other designs on the pistol *(below)* also commemorate William III, King of England and lifelong enemy of Louis, as a rival "sun king," ruling the skies as well as the land and seas.

Once on board the target ship, the pirates used axes to quickly slash through rope netting. Boarding pirates would also carry lightweight weapons, such as rapiers and small swords with long thin blades. In hand-to-hand combat, a skilled swordsman could slide the blade between the ribs of an opponent and puncture his heart or lungs. In his other hand, he might wield a smaller dagger. Cutlasses were shorter, thicker, and wider. They came in handy for chopping off limbs. They required less expertise but more physical strength. Smaller swords called for greater skill and were made for upper-class clients trained in swordsmanship.

The quartermaster led the boarding party, which included the toughest, boldest pirates. Crews that resisted were met with violence. Once aboard, pirates asked the crew for their opinion of the captain. If the report came back that he was cruel, he would be beaten, tortured, or even executed by the pirates. But if he was reported to be a captain who treated his crew well, he would likely be given one of the pirate's ships, along with some provisions, sometimes also some loot, and set free.

Pirate Weaponry

Pirates prized their weapons. They cleaned them fastidiously and kept them in good working order. Their preference was for the latest models and the best workmanship. Small arms were symbols of their outlaw status and their newly gained wealth.

In this era before mass production, every gun was individually made. Each was unique. If a part broke or was lost, it was no easy task to find a replacement. Armorers—highly skilled smiths—were essential crew members on pirate ships, needed to carry out routine maintenance and to make repairs. The quality and quantity of the weapons and spare gun parts found in the wreck suggests that the *Whydah*'s crew included an armorer.

Pirate ships were heavily armed, ready for attack or to do battle against patrolling navy vessels. Cannon provided the ship's heavy artillery. They were kept loaded and ready to fire at a moment's notice. Mounted on wooden gun carriages, they were fired from the open deck or through gun ports cut into the side of the hull below decks. Aiming and firing a cannon was no easy feat. The deck constantly shifted as the sailing ship rolled on the water. It took four to six men to operate a mounted cannon, a process that required expertise—gained in training on a navy ship or aboard a privateer—and a skill that had to be honed with lengthy drilling.

SILKEN RIBBONS

When found in the *Whydah* shipwreck, the handle of the Sun King pistol was wrapped in a silk ribbon embellished with alternating thistles and roses. Such a ribbon improved the gunman's grip. Pirates also used ribbons to hang pistols around their necks in battle.

A cannon's range was determined by the length of its barrel. The longer the barrel, the greater the velocity and impact of the ball. Cannon were categorized by the weight of the shot they fired. For example, a four-pounder fired cannonballs that weighed four pounds. When a gun founder cast a cannon, he inscribed its weight on the gun using a set of three numbers that added up, through a conventional formula, to the weight of the cannonball:

- The first number represented the quantity of hundredweight
  (1 hundredweight = 112 pounds)
- The second number represented quarters of a hundredweight (= 28 pounds)
- The third number represented pounds

If you add these together, you can calculate the cannon's weight. For example, a cannon with "3-3-1" on it weighed (3 x 112) + (3 x 28) + 1 = 421 pounds.

Navy gunners were ranked according to training and ability. In descending order, the ranks were: master gunner, gunner's mate, quarter-gunner, and gun captain.

CARPENTER'S TOOLS

Ruler, pick, hammer, and nails: tools of the trade for a carpenter, essential on any wooden vessel and hence an important asset to a pirate crew. Few ports were secure enough to allow pirates to safely repair their ships. The seaworthiness of the hull depended almost entirely on skilled carpentry.

There were two known trained gunners on the *Whydah*: Frenchman Jean Taffier, who was rescued by Bellamy in St. Croix in January 1717 after his own ship was attacked by the British Navy, and William Osborne, probably a naval deserter.

Prize Possessions

Bellamy and his crew appear to have collected large quantities of state-of-the-art firearms, judging from the remains discovered at the shipwreck. They may have intercepted these weapons as they were being shipped to French settlers and their Native American allies in Louisiana, Mississippi, and Alabama, or they might have bought them from pirate fences known to operate out of the Carolinas. Many of the firearms from the *Whydah* were customized—they were shortened, for instance, and silk ribbons were added.

Muskets took a long time to load but, at three and a half to four and a half feet long, they were also useful as clubs. Short-barreled muskets functioned as effective shotguns, primitive but deadly, at the close range offered by a ship's deck.

Eighteenth-century pistols were about one and a half feet long. Lethal when used up close to their target, these were the weapons of choice for boarding parties. A pirate might carry as many as six pistols at a time. Often these were double-shotted—each loaded with two pistol balls, giving the shooter far more firepower than a single musket would provide. Pistols were hung in a sash slung over the shoulder, keeping the hands free for fighting.

Finely handcrafted pistols were so prized that a pirate might spend the equivalent of two years' worth of a regular seaman's wages to obtain an especially fancy pair. One such pistol found in the wreckage of the *Whydah* was dubbed the Sun

VENT PICKS AND GUN WORMS

Picks and gun worms (*above, left and center*) were used to clear gunpowder residue from flintlock firearms. The picks cleared the vents and the gun worms were used with ramrods to clear the barrels. Flints (*right*) in the gunlock ignited the necessary spark.

King Pistol because of its unusual markings. Found with a silk ribbon tied around its handle and a hemp holster, the Sun King pistol has remarkable features. The mask on its escutcheon shows the Oak/Holly King, a Celtic deity with a split personality that represented winter and summer. It has a brass serpentine sideplate and a gargoyle-like sun-god design emblazoned on its butt cap.

At first glance, the sun-god design looks like many others that commemorated Louis XIV of France, known as the Sun King. But other details show that this pistol was custom-made in London. The deity on it therefore more likely represents William of Orange, who became King William III of England.

The pistol was probably commissioned by an English royalist to show his loyalty to William, who ruled England from 1689 until his death in 1702. William, an implacable enemy of Louis XIV of France, also enjoyed portraying himself as a "sun king."

Level the Deck and Change the Guard

Pirates badly wanted slave ships. They were built for speed, so that slavers could complete the Middle Passage quickly and make the most money from their cargo. They were also warships, packed with weapons—most had 12 to 24 mounted cannon. To a pirate crew seeking speed and firepower, slave ships were worthy quarry.

Slave ships were built to carry hundreds of people. This extra space was needed on a pirate ship. It created more room for the large crews, provisions, and supplies. The large galleys and industrial-size cooking pots on board slave ships could feed a hundred or more men.

Pirates wanted slave ships, but most didn't want slaves. Some had ethical objections to slavery, but more often pirates didn't want to take on the human

MAROONED

Pages 72–73: Those who broke the rule of the pirate ship's articles were marooned: left behind on an isolated island with no means of escape, as shown in this moody painting by Howard Pyle.

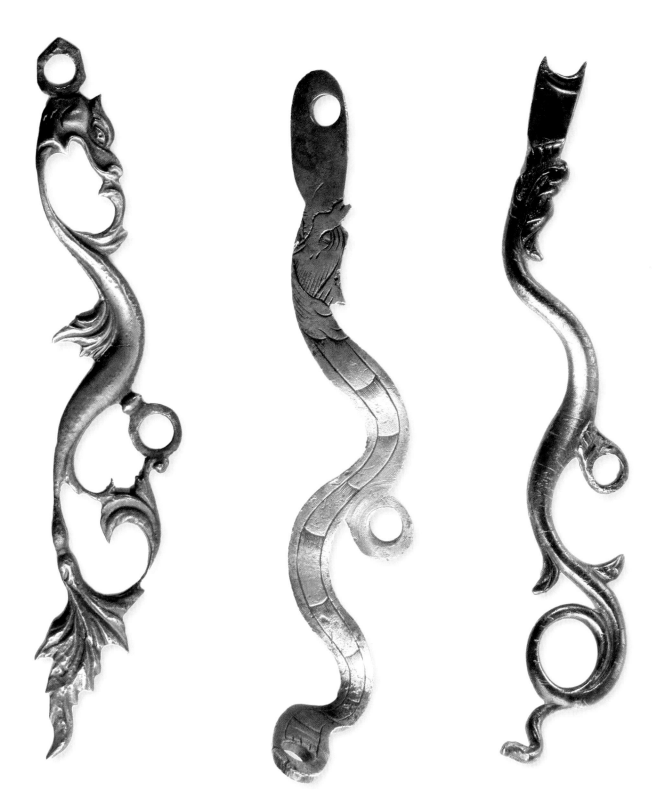

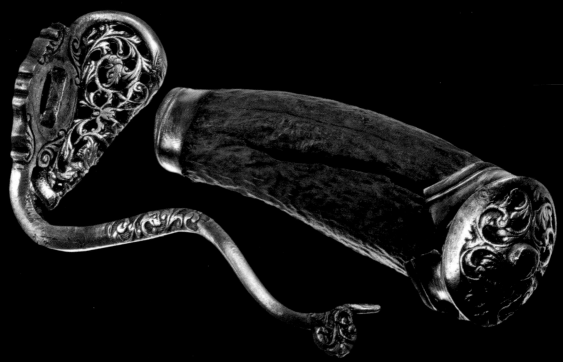

cargo because they didn't have access to slave markets. If pirates took a slave ship with captives, they often offered them the option of joining the pirate crew.

Once pirates seized a slaver, they "cleared the ship," which meant that they reconfigured the top deck of the ship, removing the forecastle, the pilot's cabin, most of the stern castle, and the barricado, the physical barrier on a slave ship that kept the captives far away from the ship's weaponry and separated them from the crew. They also lowered, or removed, the quarterdeck.

These adjustments made the ship less top heavy and more streamlined. They also provided an open fighting platform. By clearing the deck, pirates imposed a new identity on the ship: One that didn't recognize privilege, one where men elected their own captain and officers.

As soon as pirates captured a ship, they interrogated the captain. Their goal was to find out where the ship's gold, silver, and other valuables were stashed. If the captain refused to provide any information, the pirates would move on to the officers, then the crew.

Finally, if there were passengers on board, they would question them. Anyone who failed to cooperate might be brutally tortured, even killed. After the pirates had secured the loot, they stocked up on food, water, alcohol, weapons, and, if available, fine clothes.

It's a myth that pirates were only after gold, silver, and rum. They were on the lookout for other kinds of loot, too. As experienced seamen, they knew that rum and gold alone would not keep a ship with a large crew afloat and functioning for long. The other forms of booty the men needed to maintain or improve their day-to-day lives on the seas included household supplies like soap, candles, sewing tools, and galley utensils.

Pulling into a port to make repairs was no easy matter for pirates, so many repairs were made at sea. Sails and rigging were looted from captured vessels. Navigational tools, maps, and weapons were also highly prized.

REMAINS OF A SWORD

The thin blades of all the edged weapons from the *Whydah* have been eroded by the electrolytic action of saltwater through centuries underwater. Only parts of the assemblages, such as this handle and knuckle bow, remain.

Capturing the Whydah

… they spread a large black Flag, with a Death's Head and Bones across, and gave chase to Captain Prince under the same colors.

—Thomas Baker, one of Sam Bellamy's pirate crew

Sam Bellamy, aboard the *Sultana*, caught sight of the *Whydah* in the distance and set sail, chasing her relentlessly.

He followed her through the Bahamian waters for three days, and finally got close enough to capture her near Long Key, part of what is today called the Exuma Islands in the central Bahamas.

Once Bellamy and his fleet approached, Lawrence Prince, captain of the *Whydah*, put up little opposition.

It was most likely a calculated decision on the part of Prince. He knew that by offering no resistance, there was less chance that the pirates would be incited to gratuitous violence. They probably would not have fought very hard if he had ordered them to, anyway: They weren't paid enough to risk their lives for the sake of someone else's ship. They would fight, or surrender, just to save their own lives.

Once Bellamy and his men had boarded and seized the *Whydah*, there was work to be done. They spent days refitting the ship, turning it from a slaver to a pirate ship. Using smaller dinghies, they transfered booty from the *Sultana* onto their new vessel. They increased the *Whydah*'s arsenal by mounting an additional ten cannon, and they stowed two dozen more cannon in her hold.

The crew members aboard the *Whydah* were given the option of joining the pirates. A dozen did so. The rest chose to stay with Prince, and those men were set loose with him on the *Sultana*.

With that, in early 1717 the *Whydah* went from slave ship to pirate ship.

BUCCANEERS' BRAWL

Despite the apparent fight to the finish over buried treasure in Howard Pyle's 1911 illustration, the historical record shows that pirate captains and crews shared their loot in an impressively egalitarian way and were never known to have buried it in the sand.

Chapter 3

The

Pirate

Life

Like all ships' companies of the day, pirate ships were multiethnic communities—"motley crews." Pirate crews included not only sailors from all over Europe and North America but also Native Americans, Africans, and men of African descent for whom the pirate life offered an alternative to a life of slavery.

Some of these men were free men, some were runaway slaves, and some were freedmen—former slaves. Some had even worked on slaving ships. Only one early 18th-century pirate ship is known to have sailed without black crew members. Here are examples of some others:

- Blackbeard's crew was 60 percent black;
- Edward England's crew of 300 included about 80 black pirates;
- Half of John Lewis's crew of 80 were black men from English colonies;
- On his last voyage, Christopher Condent's crew of some 500 pirates included an estimated 200 black men;
- Bart Roberts's crew included 70 black men out of a total of 267; and
- Two pirate crews, the names of their commanders unknown, were almost 100 percent black.

BUTTON

Personal objects found at the *Whydah* wreck site might have belonged to crew members or been taken in plunder from other ships. A number of buttons were found, including this silver button with a colored glass inset.

Sam Bellamy's crew aboard the *Whydah* was no exception. Just consider the diversity represented by four of its crew members.

Sam Bellamy himself started out as an impoverished young English sailor, arriving in Cape Cod around 1714 to seek his fortune. After his attempt to find Spanish treasure off the coast of Florida failed, Bellamy decided to turn pirate. His career as Capt. Sam Bellamy was short but spectacular.

With him sailed Hendrick Quintor. Born in Amsterdam, Quintor was a free black man of Dutch and African descent. He was on board a Spanish brigantine in the Caribbean when it was captured by the French pirate nicknamed La Buse—The Buzzard. It didn't take Hendrick Quintor long to throw in his lot with the pirates.

Sam Bellamy counted on his shipmate John Julian, a Miskito Indian, probably born in Nicaragua or Belize. On land, Julian had no rights. But on board a pirate ship, he was valued for his navigational skills. Julian was probably around 16 years old when he became the *Whydah*'s pilot and guided it in and out of hidden harbors through the difficult waters of Cape Cod.

Also a member of Sam Bellamy's crew was John King, perhaps as young as 8 or 9. He was traveling with his mother on the Antiguan sloop *Bonetta* when she was captured by Bellamy's crew. King was determined to join the pirates. If anyone tried to stop him, he declared, he would kill himself. He even threatened his own mother. Bellamy agreed to take him on board.

Teenage pirates were not that unusual, but John King, no older than 11, is the youngest known pirate of the "Golden Age." Boys sometimes served on navy ships, working as servants to the officers or as powder monkeys, hauling gunpowder to the cannon. But pirates typically did not include young children on their crews. Somehow, young John King must have made a big impression on Sam Bellamy.

BOARDING THE WHYDAH

Pages 78–79: After a single warning shot from Bellamy's cannon, Lawrence Prince surrendered the *Whydah,* and the pirate crew proceeded to make the ship their own.

The Brotherhood

Back in the early 18th century, seamen were used to the idea of motley crews. There were at least 30 seamen of African descent on board the *Whydah* and about 20 more black pirates on the other ships in Sam Bellamy's flotilla. Bellamy's crew also included not only John Julian but at least one other Native American, whose name we do not know.

There was great solidarity and loyalty among sailors. They judged their peers by their seafaring skills. They were a brotherhood that called themselves "shipmates," "brother sailors," and "brother tars"—the term "tar" coming from their constant use of tar to patch holes in their wooden boat hulls.

Skilled black sailors were as welcome on board as any other seamen. And men with martial skills, such as African warriors, provided an intimidating presence on a boarding party.

Black men ended up on pirate ships for a number of reasons. They might be:
- former merchant sailors who had mutinied
- sailors whose ship had been taken by pirates and who decided to go on the account
- slaves who had run away from plantations
- captives on board a slave ship captured by pirates.

Even a regular black seaman could be kidnapped and sold into slavery when his ship was in port. For most black pirates, piracy offered the only alternative to slavery.

A Pirate Family Tree

Pirates rarely fought among themselves. If there were differences between crew members, they elected a second captain, split the original crew, and peacefully went their separate ways.

Pirates of the "Golden Age" formed a close-knit community with loyal bonds. A quick look at many of the age's most famous pirates reveals something like a pirate family tree.

Benjamin Hornigold ("Horn O'Gold")

Ben Hornigold was one of the founding fathers of the "Golden Age of Piracy." Sam Bellamy sailed with this veteran privateer-turned-pirate. While Hornigold—an

JOHN JULIAN

John Julian, one of the *Whydah*'s pilots, was a Miskito Indian, a group of people from southeastern Central America, the region now called the Costa de Miskitos—the Mosquito Coast—of today's Nicaragua and Honduras.

Sixteen-year-old Julian's job was to guide the ship in and out of difficult waterways. It's a little-known fact that most pirates were professional seamen. The Caribbean provides plenty of opportunities to hide, with its numerous small bays, inlets, and lagoons. When a navy ship was in pursuit, a pirate pilot with knowledge of local waterways could steer the ship to safety, taking it to a secluded spot. The pirates would stay put until they were confident that they had given the policing navy vessel the slip.

As to hanging, it is no great Hardship, for were it not for that, every cowardly Fellow would turn Pirate and so unfit the Seas, that Men of Courage must starve.　　　　　—Mary Read

Women were pirates, too. Hundreds of years ago, women didn't have a lot of working options. But then, as now, there were adventure-seeking women around. Some went to sea, often as servants, wives, or cooks. But others dressed as men and joined the army or the navy. At least a few of these women became pirates.

Mary Read ran away from home. Disguised as a man, she joined the army. Anne Bonny was disowned by her rich father when she married a sailor. The two women turned up, dressed as male sailors, on "Calico Jack" Rackham's pirate crew. The pair were so fearsome in battle that they were included in boarding parties—a job reserved for the meanest and toughest pirates.

In 1720 Mary Read and Anne Bonny were captured with the rest of their crew and put on trial. A scandalized judge sentenced the women pirates to death by hanging, but they created further surprise by revealing they were pregnant. The judge threw them both in jail, where Mary died of fever. No one knows what happened to Anne.

Englishman of an older generation—refused to attack British ships, Bellamy felt no such allegiance. In the summer of 1716, the younger, ambitious Sam Bellamy split from Hornigold and struck out on his own.

Henry Jennings

In 1715, Henry Jennings obtained a Jamaican privateering license that authorized attacks on certain Spanish shipping. When the politics changed and the license was revoked, Jennings turned pirate. He led a raid on the fort where the treasure recovered from the sunken Spanish fleet was held, igniting this age of piracy. Bellamy got his start as a pirate by working with Jennings.

La Buse ("The Buzzard")

A French pirate who went by many names, La Buse joined the Hornigold-Bellamy flotilla in 1716. When Bellamy split from Hornigold, La Buse went along with him for a few months. In July 1717, after the shipwreck of the *Whydah,* La Buse and Palgrave Williams joined forces in the Carolinas. When the authorities in the Caribbean began to crack down, the pair worked the African coast.

Edward Teach ("Blackbeard")

Many are familiar with the infamous pirate called Blackbeard. Like Bellamy, he sailed for a while with Hornigold. Blackbeard's fearsome appearance struck terror in the hearts of his victims. With his long black beard twisted up with ribbons, he wore a sling with holsters, each with a pistol inside. Ruthless and cruel, even his own crew were afraid of him.

Stede Bonnet

Bonnet was a gentleman pirate, coming from a rich family that owned a large plantation in Barbados. Although he had no experience at sea, Bonnet managed

BLACKBEARD

Edward Teach became Blackbeard, a larger-than-life character whose adventures have thrilled generations of writers and painters. He would charge into battle with lit matches tucked under his cap. His death at the hands of the Royal Navy in 1718 was seen as a major victory in the war against pirates.

STEDE BONNET

HOWELL DAVIS

CHARLES VANE

a few lucrative raids before he joined forces with Blackbeard. It didn't take Blackbeard long to realize that Bonnet was incompetent, however, and he soon put one of his own men in command of Bonnet's ship.

Charles Vane

Vane took more than 50 prizes in his career. He showed little mercy to his victims. When he refused to attack a French ship, his men accused him of being a coward and voted to replace him with their quartermaster, Jack Rackham. Vane's disgrace was short-lived, as he soon managed to work his way back up to captain.

Howell Davis

Welshman Davis became a pirate when the slave ship he worked on was captured by the Irish pirate Edward England. After basing himself in the Caribbean for a while, Davis moved his center of operations to the West African coast. Bart Roberts turned pirate when the slave ship on which he was a mate was captured by Davis.

Jack Rackham ("Calico Jack")

Rackham was promoted to captain on board Charles Vane's ship when Vane refused to attack a French ship. Because of his colorful clothes, Rackham was known as "Calico Jack." He only sailed small sloops, and he treated his victims with respect. His crew included the women pirates, Anne Bonny and Mary Read.

Bartholomew Roberts ("Black Bart")

"Black Bart" Roberts was perhaps the most successful pirate of his time. He captured more than 400 ships between 1719 and 1722 and commanded a fleet of more than 500 men. A fearless and disciplined leader and a teetotaler, Roberts outlawed gambling on his ship. When he turned pirate, Roberts claimed he wanted "a short life and a merry one."

The Ship's Articles

A ship's articles were the code of conduct, agreed to and signed by everyone who wanted to join a pirate crew. New recruits took part in a ceremony that included the whole crew and plenty of liquor. They swore an oath of loyalty and agreed never to betray or cheat their shipmates.

According to testimony from Bart Roberts's crew, his recruits signed the articles at night. They were led into his ship's great cabin by candlelight and presented with the articles and a loaded pistol, laid together on a platter. The implication was that the recruit could chose between the two.

Other trial testimony revealed that recruits faced a mirror as they swore their oath to the articles. At the time, mirrors were believed to provide an avenue to the next world. A pact made before a mirror was not to be taken lightly.

Once a pirate had signed the articles, he had an equal vote, an equal share of the booty, and the chance to be elected as an officer. These rights extended to everyone on board—black, white, and Indian. To poor, disenfranchised men and women of all colors, pirate ships were islands of freedom in a world of few options. It is little surprise that, given the opportunity, they often chose to sign the articles and go on the account.

Not everyone joined a pirate ship willingly, however. Men with specialist skills, such as carpenters, navigators, and doctors, were highly valued on all ships. Pirates referred to them as "artists" and forced them to sign the articles under threat of death if they refused to enlist willingly.

This happened to Thomas Davis, a Welsh shipwright, when Bellamy seized his ship, the *St. Michael*, off St. Croix in December 1716. A trained carpenter was essential on any ship to oversee the constant maintenance needed by a wooden vessel. When Bellamy's crew captured the *St. Michael*, they needed a carpenter. They refused to take "No" for an answer and forced Davis to sign up as a pirate.

Captain Bartholomew Roberts's Ship's Articles

EVERY MAN Sworne by Book & Mirror to be true to these Articles, & to his Ship Mates, is to have a Vote in Matters of Importance. He who is not Sworne, shall not Vote.

EVERY MAN to have Equal Right to ye Provisions or Liquors at any time & to use them at Pleasure, unless Scarcity makes a Restriction necessary for ye Good of All.

EVERY MAN to be called ffairly a Board Prizes in turn by the List of ye Company. Every Boarder is to have a Suit of Cloaths from ye Prize.

THE CAPTAIN & Officers are to be chosen on Commencement of a Voyage, & on any other Occasion as ye Company shall deeme fit.

THE POWER of ye Captain is Supream in Chace or Battle. He may beat, cut, or shoot any who dares Deny his Command on such Occasions. In all other Matters whatsoever he is to be Governed by the Will of ye Company.

EVERY MAN shall obey Civill Command.

HE WHO first sees a Sail, shall have ye best Pistol, or Small Arm, from a Board her.

YE QUARTER=Master shall be first a Board any Prize. He is to separate for ye Company's Use what he sees fit & shall have Trust of ye Common Stock & Treasurey until it be Shared. He shall Keep a Book shewing each Man's Share, & each Man may draw from ye Common Stock & Treasurey against his Share upon Request.

ANY MAN who should Defraud ye Company, or another, to ye Vallew of a Dollar, he shall suffer Punishment as ye Company deeme ffit.

EACH MAN to keep his Musket, Pistolls, & Cutlass cleane & ffit for Service, upon Inspection by ye Quarter=Master.

NO PRUDENT Woman, or Boy, is to be brought a board. No Married Man is to be fforced to serve our Company.

GOOD QUARTERS to be Granted when Called for.

ANY MAN who Deserts ye Company, keeps any Secret, or Deserts his Station in Time of Battle, shall be punished by Death, Marooning, or Whipping, as ye Company shall deeme ffit & Just.

NOT A WORD shall be Written by any Man unless it be nailed Publickly to ye Mast.

—from *Capt. Charles Johnson's A General History of the Pyrates*, 1724

Life On Board a Pirate Ship

The musicians to have rest on the Sabbath Day, but the other six days and nights, none have special favor.

—from Black Bart Roberts's ship's articles

QUARRY ESCAPES

Following pages: Pirates as imagined by 20th-century artist Bernard Finegan Gribble watch a targeted ship sail out of their reach, leaving their rail blasted by cannon shot.

Pirate ships were cosmopolitan with large crews. There were more than 150 men on the *Whydah* when she sank, for example. The men on board were English, Irish, Native American, African (or of African descent), Scottish, Welsh, French, Dutch, Spanish, and Swedish. They called themselves "Robin Hood's Men"—they were united in a common enterprise that cut across the usual boundaries of nationality and religion.

Like most pirates—and indeed like most regular seamen of those days—Sam Bellamy and the men of his pirate crew were mostly in their 20s, and most came from humble backgrounds. But unlike regular sailors, pirates controlled their own destiny, electing their own officers, establishing their ship's course, and sharing the loot.

Even on a pirate ship, a certain level of discipline was necessary. Large crews eased the workload, but the men still needed to

PISSOIR

The ship's toilet, also called a "pissdale," consisted of two lead tubes, one in the head and another in the stern.

TABLE SETTING

Seamen of the early 18th century had personal utensils that they owned or were responsible for. Several pewter plates inscribed with the initials of their pirate owners have been found at the *Whydah* site. One pewter plate *(above)* was inscribed with a crosshatched flag design *(right)*, which may have been intended as the British Union Jack.

keep a constant watch on the weather and deploy all their seamanship skills. They were moving through difficult, often uncharted waters, traveling long distances as they chased prey or evaded capture by navy vessels.

Though pirates came from many places, the nationality of the ship would determine its language. On a French ship, for instance, everyone communicated in French. The majority of pirates were from the British Isles, and the main language spoken on the *Whydah,* as on most pirate ships, was English. Many Africans at this time were familiar with Pidgin English and could communicate in English.

Although large crews meant less work, living on the seas in cramped, damp, cold conditions was reason enough for staying merry. Pirates drank anything they could get their hands on. Rum, of course, was predominant, often watered down and known as grog. But pirates also liked to drink brandy; wines like Madeira, port, and claret; and different types of "punch"—liquor mixed with wine, sugar, water, and flavorings.

Some ships of the day had small bands and orchestras. Sailors whiled away the hours on long voyages by singing and dancing. Any musicians captured by pirates were compelled to sign the ship's articles. Trumpeters, pipers, drummers, fiddlers, harpists, and flutists would play on deck during boarding parties, and below deck for the entertainment of the crew.

Pirates even performed plays on ships. The *Whydah* crew staged a play about a mock pirate trial, called *The Royal Pirate.* A group of crew members, the worse for drink, missed the first act. They stumbled in—clueless that a play was being performed—just as one of the actors was being sentenced to death for piracy.

Outraged, they leapt to his defense, throwing hand grenades and drawing their cutlasses, breaking

CUFFLINKS

Pirates liked to mimic the style of fashionable gentlemen. Copper cufflinks recovered from the *Whydah* may have been booty given to a pirate after he boarded a ship. Members of a boarding party got first choice among the clothes they found on the captured ship.

GOLD RING

Crudely engraved, this gold ring has been the subject of much conjecture. Some believe that the cryptic letters stand for a Welsh good luck wish, while others believe they spell the name of a Royal Navy seaman who turned pirate.

CLAY PIPE

Opposite: A bowl of tobacco and a good story were always a comfort aboard any ship. Even in the 1700s there were smoking regulations: No pirate was allowed belowdecks with a lit pipe after dark, for fear of fire.

the actor's leg, taking the arm off the playwright, and killing a member of the audience.

Some ships' articles prohibited gambling, but most pirates gambled as hard as they drank. They bet on games like backgammon, cards, checkers, and dice. In 1703, Capt. Woodes Rogers' crew signed a declaration to give up all gambling after some had wagered and lost all their personal possessions, including their clothes.

Life on a navy or merchant ship was physically demanding. Men worked long hours in all weather and were chronically underfed. A group of six to nine men might share a bucket of meat and a tray of ship's biscuits, which might be infested with weevils or maggots. The only utensils sailors used were their knives. They would dip a biscuit into a bucket and scoop out the meat, along with some juice, using the biscuit as their plate.

But on a pirate ship, each man had his own utensils. Some of the plates recovered from the *Whydah* were marked with the pirates' personal signatures. Pirates enjoyed a more varied diet than naval or merchant ship sailors. Their meals included food and drink from looted ships as well as fish, turtles, and birds that they caught in their free time.

Putting on Airs

Most pirates, like other sailors of the day, came from humble origins and dressed plainly. But some defied their social status and dressed in looted finery, exotic clothes of vivid satin, silk, and velvet plundered from their prizes. When they could, they paraded in high style, wearing fashion accessories like the brass buttons and silver cufflinks recovered from the *Whydah*.

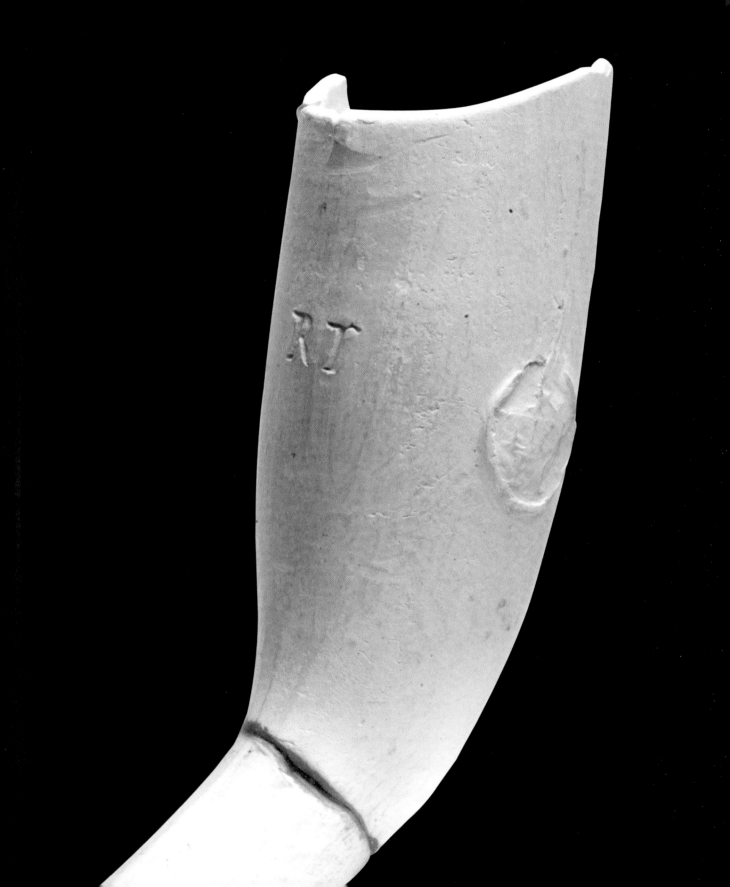

A. DEBELLE DEL.

A. CATEL SC.

Pirates divided the gold and silver they took equally, but members of boarding parties could keep the clothing looted from the passengers and crew of captured vessels. Captains liked to mimic the high fashion worn by merchant ship captains.

One interesting personal item found among the *Whydah* artifacts was a gold ring with unusual markings on it, including the word "Teye" and the letter combinations "BA" and "WFS." There is much speculation about their meaning. Here's one possible explanation:

- "Teye" is a last name from the north of England.
- "BA" might refer to the able-bodied seaman's certification—an important milestone in a sailor's career.
- "WFS" could indicate "Western Fleet Station," a Royal Navy base at Kingston, Jamaica.

In 1715—after the Spanish fleet was wrecked off the coast of Florida—many sailors from the Western Fleet Station deserted to hunt treasure. Some of these men turned pirate. This ring may have belonged to a naval seaman named Teye who became a pirate.

ROMANTIC REPUTATION

This romanticized image of a corsair and his adoring wench is typical of pirate mythology—but far from true. Pirates of the early 18th century rarely allowed women aboard their ships, believing them to bring bad luck.

Staying the Course

In this ship, the 'Rosario,' we took also a great book full of sea-charts and maps, containing a very accurate and exact description of all the ports, soundings, creeks, rivers, capes, and coasts belonging to the South Sea, and all the navigations usually performed by the Spaniards in that ocean.

—William Dick, pirate

In order to control the seas, you first had to know how to navigate them. The Spanish were the first Europeans to chart the waters of the New World.

Sea maps, always at a premium, were created on board during voyages. Back in Europe, the maps were copied for compatriots. When the English buccaneer Capt. Bartholomew Sharp and his crew captured the Spanish ship *El Santo Rosario* in 1681, they knew the value of the detailed and extensive sea charts and maps they found on board. In an early act of industrial espionage, they took them back to England, where they were presented to the King. He responded by granting pardons to Sharp and his crew. The maps were translated and used by English shipping and military.

On a merchant ship, the primary person to read and interpret such maps would be the sailing master, second in command to the captain. On board a pirate ship, his sole responsibility was the navigation of the ship. The *Whydah's* sailing master was an Englishman, John Lambert.

Navigational methods and calculations were primitive. Sea charts were inadequate or, for some regions, even nonexistent. A skilled navigator could calculate latitude—the distance north or south of the Equator—to within ten miles. But calculations of longitude—the distance east or west of a line called the prime meridian that runs through Greenwich, England—were often inaccurate. Errors of longitude in the early 18th century could amount to hundreds of miles.

Most of the time a ship would leave port and sail in a northerly or southerly direction, depending on the latitude of her destination. Once the ship reached the correct latitude, the captain and sailing master would turn the boat 90 degrees and attempt to set sail due east or due west, staying as close to the desired course as possible.

The course of a pirate ship was decided by a vote. Every crewman participated in working the ship during a cruise. Once the course was set, the boatswain—or bosun—would supervise the crew as they set and struck the ship's sails, maintained the rigging, handled the cargo, hauled in the lines, and weighed the anchors.

Irishman Jeremiah Burke was the bosun on board the *Whydah*. To get elected to that job, Burke would have been one of the most experienced and capable members of the crew.

SPIGOT

A brass spigot like this was probably used on casks of wine and stored near the ship's galley.

The boatswain helped to mete out punishment, too, such as a flogging, ordered if there was ever any infringement of the ship's articles.

On a pirate ship, the captain had no special privileges. It was only in battle that his authority was unquestioned. The quartermaster was as important as the captain and a check on his power. Because his duties required some bookwork, he was probably literate, unlike most sailors, who could barely scrawl their own names.

Richard Noland, the *Whydah*'s quartermaster, came from Dublin, Ireland. He was a veteran pirate on Benjamin Hornigold's crew before joining Bellamy.

As quartermaster, Noland's responsibilities included representing the crew on issues that concerned their welfare, settling minor disputes and dispensing punishment if required, leading the attack when pirates boarded a ship, taking command of captured prizes, and managing and distributing the stolen loot.

Keeping Everything Shipshape

If you were going to spend days on end outrunning navy vessels or pursuing fast prizes, your ship had to be in top condition. To maintain her seaworthiness, pirates would careen the ship—run her ashore to work on the hull out of the water—a process overseen by the ship's carpenter that required extensive

In the 1600s, a ship's captain registered the death of a crewman by flying a plain black flag. He also entered a skull and crossbones—a death's head, commonly used on gravestones—beside the dead man's name in the ship's log. Today, the skull and crossbones symbolize death and danger. They have been borrowed for medical usage to indicate poison. To pirates, though, the image spoke of their strength and suggested resurrection and rebirth.

Pirates created the Jolly Roger by combining the black flag with the skull and crossbones. Most pirate ships flew some variation of this flag—a black background with symbolic figures outlined in white or sometimes red. Some flags included other symbols: An hourglass represented the swift passage of time, for example. A wounded heart

Swords or cutlasses spoke a threat of violence.

most likely signified danger. Cutlasses, swords, or "darts of death" implied weapons and spoke a threat of violence.

The Jolly Roger was a symbol of unity and defiance. When it was hoisted, the crew fired their weapons, saluted their captain and themselves, and set out on the hunt for prey. "A merry life but a short one!"

Ships of the day flew many different kinds of flags, including national flags. By flying the Jolly Roger, pirates were proclaiming themselves outlaws, citizens of no nation. As outlaws, pirates had no rights under the law. They could be killed with impunity. If they were convicted at trial, they were hanged. No wonder that they chose to sail under "King Death," the Jolly Roger.

knowledge, efficiency, skill, and speed. While careening the ship, pirates were vulnerable to attack by enemies.

Several times a year, the crew would find a secluded beach in an isolated cove that they considered a fit place for them to run the ship safely ashore. They would turn her on her side, secure her, and then carefully scrape the algae, seaweed, and barnacles from the bottom of her hull.

If repairs were needed—if planks in the hull had to be replaced—the crew would take care of them. Seams were caulked with oakum and pitch. Damaged areas might be covered with strips of lead sheeting to make the ship watertight before raising her and setting back out to sea.

> *No man will be a sailor who has contrivance enough to get himself into a jail; for being in a ship is being in a jail, with the chance of being drowned … A man in a jail has more room, better food, and commonly better company.*
>
> —Samuel Johnson

The rough wear and tear on a wooden ship made constant work for the ship's carpenter. Once pirates took a ship, the carpenter and gunners would set to work, modifying it immediately. Bulkheads—internal walls—were removed belowdecks to create space for additional cannon and to make more living space for the large pirate crew.

When Bellamy seized the *Whydah* and turned it from a slave ship into a pirate ship, the ship's carpenter, working with helpers, had to dismantle the remnants of the slave quarters—in reality no more than a temporary platform, or shelf, that was installed halfway up the belowdecks area. In a slave ship, the captives had to lie on the hard planks. They were squeezed together as closely as possible, in two tiers, one platform above the other.

LIFE ON BOARD

Following pages: An imagined moment of leisure, this engraving does show the larger size of pirate crews than those aboard naval or merchant vessels. Pirates fooled their victims into thinking there were fewer sailors on board. Some dressed as women, to look like regular passengers.

TEA KETTLE

After only a short time at sea, stored fresh water frequently stank and squirmed with aquatic organisms (such as small red worms). Hence, even boiled, it was generally reserved for cooking.

On a merchant or navy ship, the officers slept in relative comfort in cabins, while the crew slept in cramped quarters belowdecks. Pirates often leveled the top deck, removing most of the cabins. The captain of a pirate ship was expected to share his food, his drink, and even the great cabin with the crew. If the men so wished, they slept in the cabin. In a typical gesture of pirate democracy, everyone slept in a hammock—but only if there were enough to go around. If not, all slept on deck.

Surgeons & Freemasons

If any Man should lose a Limb, or become a Cripple, he is to have 800 Dollars out of ye Common Stock, & for lesser hurts, Proportionably.

　　　　　　　　—from Capt. Bartholomew Roberts's ship's articles

Scurvy—caused by vitamin C deficiency—was widespread on all ships. Victims lost their teeth and had to stop eating altogether when the disease destroyed their gum tissue.

The on-board freshwater supply was often contaminated, resulting in outbreaks of typhus or dysentery. Malaria, smallpox, and tuberculosis were common. And the extreme damp and lack of heating promoted asthma, consumption, and rheumatoid arthritis.

The ship's surgeon took care of battle wounds. Injured limbs were amputated without the help of antibiotics or anesthetics. The doctor held the limb under his arm and sawed it off as quickly as possible. He tied off the arteries or cauterized the stump with a red-hot broadaxe. If there was no doctor on board, the ship's carpenter handled the job.

TOOLS FOR NAVIGATION

These brass dividers would have been used by the ship's sailing master to measure distance on maps and charts, plotting course and direction.

James Ferguson, the surgeon on board the *Whydah*, was from Paisley, Scotland. He was probably a political fugitive who had taken part in the failed Jacobite revolt in 1715 against the German-born King George I.

Some pirates from the British Isles were known to be Jacobites, rebels who fought against the English crown. As a result of their political activity, many were sent to the Caribbean as indentured servants.

Others fled there before they could be arrested. Men from both groups ended up on pirate ships. Their political allegiance was sometimes reflected in the names of their ships—an example is the ship commanded by Howell Davis, known by the name *King James.*

A pewter plate found in the wreckage of the *Whydah* suggests that the crew may have included Jacobites. Inscribed on the top of the plate, near the rim, may be the oldest reliably dated representation of the hallmark of the fraternal order of Freemasons. How did this come to be carved on a pirate's dinner plate?

A number of Jacobites belonged to Masonic lodges. This mysterious inscription was probably a result of direct contact between Bellamy's pirates and one or more Jacobite supporters who were also Masons.

The unusual crosshatched design on the bowl of a spoon found in the shipwreck may represent a Masonic cable-tow. A rope with loops at both ends symbolizes a vow of duty and obligation by which a man pledged his life to the Freemasons and which bound the order of Freemasons to the individual member. The presence of a quality mark, an "X," on the spoon suggests it was made in England after 1690. The etched initials, "E.H.," are most likely those of the original owner.

Pirate Myths

What about buried treasure? On this subject, as on many others, it is interesting to separate myths and fiction from history.

Most stories about buried pirate treasure were inspired by the fact that the notorious Captain Kidd is known to have tried hard to conceal his treasure from the authorities.

In reality, however, most pirates didn't keep their treasure long enough to bury it. They gambled or drank their ill-gotten gains as soon as the opportunity presented itself. A few, who successfully retired from their lives of crime, even

DIVIDING THE TREASURE

Some of our strongest ideas about
pirates have little to do with historical
reality. They come from books, films,
and paintings by artists like Howard
Pyle, who—inspired by the stories and
rumors—created larger-than-life figures
from his imagination, as in this painting.

FORK

The only example of a pewter fork
found thus far at the *Whydah* site, this
four-tined fork appears to have been
manufactured between the late 1660s
and 1700. An incised crest shows a
seated primate in a floral-crested shield.

used their shares of loot to start up legitimate enterprises. While there are few documented instances of pirates burying treasure, far more money has been spent looking for it than has ever been found.

There isn't much basis in the stories of pirates making their victims walk the plank, either. The only known instance comes from the Caribbean in 1829—long after the "Golden Age" was over. If pirates wanted to get rid of someone, they would just throw him overboard while out to sea.

Historical and archaeological studies of the *Whydah*, and other pirate ships, demonstrate that truth is stranger than fiction when it comes to pirates.

KETTLE HANDLES

Iron kettles and pots were essential for boiling the sailors' food and water, but the relatively thin material of most has eroded away underwater over these three centuries. These brass handles from a kettle did survive, however.

Real Pirate Treasure

20,000 or 30,000 pounds sterling, was counted over, in the cabin, and put up in bags, fifty pounds weight to every man's share, there being 180 men on board.
—trial testimony of Peter Hoof, *Whydah* crew member

Pirate treasure was not just a myth, however. Pirates did seize enormous amounts of precious metals and huge numbers of coins. The potential wealth involved was without doubt one of the attractions of the pirate life.

A merchant sailor worked long days. He was often treated harshly, usually badly fed, and paid meager wages. Often he received less than he'd been promised; sometimes he was paid nothing at all. But a sailor who turned pirate and went on the account became a shareholder in the ship's company. Each man on board a pirate ship received a cut of the ship's booty, or plunder. His share, or account, was calculated as a proportion of all the loot seized in the course of a cruise.

Like regular sailors, pirates didn't risk carrying their stashes of coins around with them in wallets or purses. They had to come up with solutions to keep it more secure.

They might roll their coins into the top of their stockings or even sew them into the lining of a vest or waistcoat.

Or they might drill holes in the coins and thread them through a leather thong to make a bracelet or necklace.

Instead of the loot being doled out to each crew member aboard, it was often put into a common chest, supervised, controlled, and distributed later by the quartermaster.

The quartermaster would manage the common booty through an accounting system that could become quite complicated. In an early version of social security, for example, crew members were paid compensation out of the common chest for wounds sustained. Such payments were made before the general division of the loot, and there was at least one instance in which a piratical common chest was thereby bankrupted.

Once compensations for injury were made, here is an example of how the remaining loot was divided:

- 1 share to each regular member of the crew
- 2 shares each to the quartermaster and captain
- 1½ shares to the sailing master, boatswain, and surgeon
- 1¼ shares to the other officers.

Aboard merchant and naval ships, the difference in pay between the top and the bottom of the hierarchy was far greater, and this made for resentment among men who believed that equal risk should make for equal pay. Pirates knew that their commonly shared risk and equal pay galled the common

WRITING INSTRUMENTS

As chief record keeper, the quartermaster would have used this inkwell and pens. Each pen would have held a nib, writing either with ink or lead.

TEARDROP-SHAPED COIN

Opposite: During the 17th and 18th centuries, Spanish colonial mints clipped coin-sized slices from flat strips of silver, embossed with the royal coat of arms and the cross of Spain. If they were overweight, the excess was clipped off. No two coins were exactly alike.

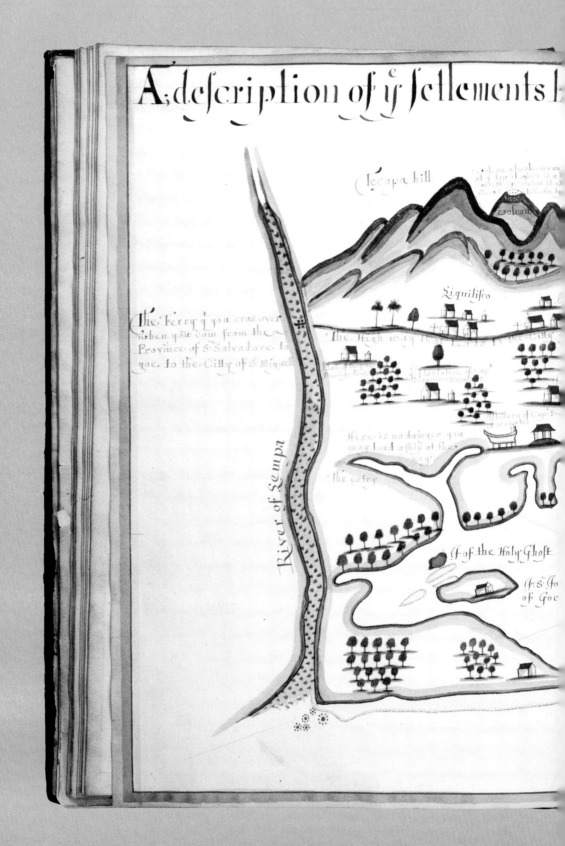

Tecapa hill

Volcan

Tiquilisco

The Ferry yᵗ you cros over
when you com from the
Province of Sᵗ Salvadore to
goe to the Citty of Sᵗ Miquel

The High way

Here is no danger you
may load a ship at the
key

the entry

of the Holy Ghost

of Sᵗ Jo
of Goc

River of Lempa

The map contains the following hand-lettered labels:

cen ij R. lempa & ij of S. miguell

S: Miguell
Monte Mendeo
Point
Assistant Hill
Joseph Mario worke
S: Mary
S: Miguell
Officion
Palmarias
Canoas Passage
Isle of
To this place, you may bring a ship of 200 tunns Burthen & load
the River of S: miguell has 8 fathom water
Isle of
Bar of Gibaltique
Socorran

SEA CHART

Because many seas and lands were still uncharted, maps were highly prized. Pirates would have been on the lookout for them when they sacked a prize. This colorful interpretation of a Caribbean coastline was seized as plunder when Bartholomew Sharp and his crew captured the Spanish ship *El Santo Rosario*.

sailor, and they used their own way of dividing the loot as a lure to recruit new pirates. Pirates were so insistent on equality that even valuable gold jewelry was broken up into tiny fragments, with a hammer on a cutting stone, so that the pieces could be equally divided by weight.

When pickings were slim, the quartermaster would count out the coins to each crew member. After a bonanza, shares were measured out in pounds, bowls, or hatfuls.

Pirate ships carried troy weights, used to measure small amounts of gold. The smallest unit of weight, a drachma, equaled about 1.944 grams, or one-sixteenth of a troy ounce. According to British law, all weights had to be marked with a "G" and a Crown design, certifying that they matched standard measurements. And although they were supposed to be tested, this was rare. A set of weights found from the *Whydah*, for example, measured 9.5 grams less than its marked weight.

Gold, Silver, and Coins

When the *Whydah* sank, she was carrying booty plundered from more than 50 ships. There was a fortune on board in gold and silver, plus other goods that could be sold to pirate "fences" for cash—items like elephant tusks, cloth, sugar, and indigo, commodities drawn from across the Atlantic world. Each pirate would share in the proceeds of the sale.

Gold bars found on the *Whydah* show signs of having been scored with a knife to make sure they were real gold and not just lead bars with a gold coating. Pirates made homemade bars of silver by melting down looted ornaments. Silver and gold bars were easier to carry and to divide among the crew.

The *Whydah's* cargo also included treasure from Potosí, a mountain in today's Bolivia from which precious metals were mined. At Potosí, Indian laborers were

NESTED SCALE WEIGHTS

Troy weights like these were used to measure small amounts of gold. The number 4 on the outer cup indicates four troy ounces. Twelve troy ounces equal one pound. The crossed tulips, rosebuds, and the initials "W.H." are brand marks identifying the weights' maker.

TREASURE!

Thousands of coins have been found
in the *Whydah* shipwreck. Many were
pieces of eight, the closest thing to
a universal coinage in the Atlantic
world at the time.

forced to hammer silver ore loose from rock walls in dangerous mine shafts, some as deep as 900 feet. They heaved the silver in baskets through narrow tunnels to the surface, where it was ground into fine powder. The silver was combined with mercury and the mixture cooked until the mercury boiled off. Then it was cast into bars from which coin-sized slices were cut off.

The coins were minted into denominations weighing one-half, one, two, four, and eight *reales*, a Spanish unit of weight. Coins weighing eight reales were called "pieces of eight." The cross of Spain was embossed on one side of the coin, the royal coat of arms on the other. Each coin was weighed and, if its weight went over the standard, the extra metal was cut off. No two coins were exactly alike.

COINS

Coins of 18th-century Spain were valued by weight, their edges clipped to meet the required measurement. Pieces of eight *(opposite, upper right)* weighed eight *reales,* a common unit.

Silver was carried down the high Andean mountain trails on llamas on a two-week trip to the port of Arica on the Pacific coast. From there, the treasure was freighted north in small vessels to Callao, the port for the city of Lima, Peru, from where it was carried to the city of Panama. The treasure was then transported across the isthmus of Panama either entirely overland by mule on dangerous mountain trails, or partly by water down the Chagres River, to the Caribbean port city of Portobello.

Every Coin Tells a Story

If any Man shall lose a Joint in Time of an Engagement, he shall have 400 Pieces of Eight, if a Limb, 800.

—From Capt. John Phillips' ship's articles

Pieces of eight, the most famous coins from the age of piracy, were the closest thing to a global currency at the time. Each piece of eight weighed eight

reales, a little more than an English ounce. Thirty-two of these one-real Spanish silver coins were equal to one 18th-century British pound sterling. A pound and a half sterling per month, or six pieces of eight, was the going wage for a sailor between 1713 and 1725. One Spanish piece of eight, found in the shipwreck of the *Whydah*, showed "53," indicating that the coin was minted in 1653, the year that French buccaneer Jean Le Vasseur was murdered.

Le Vasseur was the primary founder of Tortuga, the buccaneer stronghold off the northwestern coast of Hispaniola. A former military engineer, Le Vasseur built Tortuga's infamous crow's-nest fortress, Fort de Rocher. From this vantage point, the buccaneers fought off repeated Spanish attempts to defeat them and take the island.

WOUNDED HEART SEAL

With an imprint cruder than that found on a silver seal, a brass seal *(above)* is more likely to have been used by a common sailor than by a captain or officer to seal a letter. Objects such as the seal *(right)* lodged for centuries underwater.

Numerous coins were found in the wreckage of the *Whydah:* a French silver half-ecu, for example, worth about two shillings three pence in the British currency of the day. Minted in Paris in 1691—during the reign of Louis XIV—the coin recalls the exploits of English buccaneer and explorer William Dampier, who became in that very year the first man to circumnavigate the globe twice. He went on to complete a third circumnavigation in 1710. Possessed of exceptional observational skills, Dampier was both an outstanding navigator and an accomplished scientist. His books, *A New Voyage Round the World* and *A Voyage to New Holland,* were prized by explorers, navigators, and naturalists. In great detail, he described his routes, innovative navigational methods, and the unfamiliar birds and animals he saw on his travels. More than a century later, Charles Darwin used Dampier's books for reference on his voyage on the *Beagle.*

Spanish silver, looted from the New World, drove the economy of early modern Europe. Some coins pictured the powerful Charles V, son of Ferdinand and Isabella, King of Spain and other lands and, from 1530 to 1558, Holy Roman Emperor. Charles proudly declared that he ruled over an empire on which the sun never set. Charles' territories included all, or part of, the modern countries of Spain, Italy, the Netherlands, Austria, Luxemburg, Germany, Belgium, Switzerland, France, and colonial possessions in the New World, extending from Mexico and the Caribbean basin south to Peru. His lands even stretched across the Pacific to the Philippines.

1697 was the year of the great raid on Cartagena, Colombia—the mightiest fortress in Spanish colonial America. Engaged in a desperate struggle with the Spanish during the War of the Grand Alliance, the French naval admiral Baron de Pointis recruited 600 buccaneers at Hispaniola to help him take the fortress and its treasure, estimated to equal 10 to 20 million pounds sterling in value.

De Pointis promptly cheated the surviving buccaneers out of their share of the booty and returned to France. He presented King Louis XIV with treasure worth two million pounds. This raid marked a halt to piracy and buccaneering in the Caribbean until the Spanish treasure fleet sank in 1715.

GOLD INGOTS

Melted and molded into portable chunks, these gold ingots reveal score marks made with a knife, where pirates had tested them to make sure they were solid gold, not just gold-coated lead.

A WATERY GRAVE

Opposite: When the *Whydah* sank, its treasure plunged to the bottom of the ocean.

To Seal Their Fate

Seals were common in the 1700s, so it is not surprising that among the *Whydah* treasure there would be a few. In those days, letters were folded and closed with melted candle wax, which was then stamped with the sender's seal. The design carved on the seal left an impression on the wax. Seals sometimes included the sender's initials. Images and symbols communicated ideas. A seal also served as a signature in a society in which many people were illiterate. Pirates who couldn't read or write might use their seals to sign the articles.

One seal found among the *Whydah* wreckage contains a pair of turtle doves, a symbol of romantic love. The ocean between them implies separation by a sea

BURYING THE TREASURE

Artist Howard Pyle's powerful images have resulted in the widespread belief that pirates buried their treasure in the Caribbean sand. The historical record does not support the legend.

voyage. The balance scales—often a symbol of the hand of fate—often represent danger, but on this seal a laurel wreath surrounds them. The wreath may represent the hopes shared by lovers, who yearn to be reunited despite hazards ahead.

The French inscription on the seal means: "Death, if I lose you." The quality and the choice of silver as the material for this seal both suggest that it was made for a particularly well-to-do buyer.

Another seal found on the *Whydah* was less fancy, made of brass, with a cruder engraving, but its design was even more intriguing. The heart pierced with arrows can signify a lost love, but it also implies mortal danger. The symbol at the top might represent a Celtic pagan sun god, or it may stand for the constant star that safely guides sailors through danger and provides heavenly protection against hazards and foes.

The waxing and waning moons on the bottom of the design might represent monthly cycles of fertility. Crescent moons are also, however, a common symbol Islamic design element. The design of the post, or handle, of this seal is reminiscent of Moroccan designs. Many English, French, and Spanish *renegados*—rebels—joined forces with the Muslim corsairs of the time.

homeward Bound

With the *Whydah* as his new flagship, Capt. Sam Bellamy led a fearsome pirate flotilla, seizing ships and plundering them for their riches. By the time the fleet reached New England, each man was due at least one 50-pound sack of treasure.

The crew must have whiled away many hours talking of their plans to spend this great wealth. Soon the treasure—and nearly all the men—had sunk to the bottom of the ocean.

Chapter 4

The **Whydah**

Lost & Found

In March 1717 Sam Bellamy sailed south from the Bahamas. Near Gonaive, on the Haitian coast, he seized the richly laden *Tanner Frigate*. Frenchman Jean Shuan joined Bellamy's crew. From Gonaive, the pirates turned northward to head back up the North American coast. Off the Delaware capes, Bellamy took half a dozen ships.

GRINDSTONE

Operated by a hand-crank, a grindstone was essential equipment on board the *Whydah*. The carpenter had many tools that needed to be kept sharp. The grindstone was also used to sharpen blades on weapons and kitchen knives.

Continuing up the Atlantic coast—en route for Cape Elizabeth on the coast of Maine—Bellamy turned toward Cape Cod on April 26. Legend has it that he intended to pick up Maria Hallett. Palgrave Williams, on the *Marianne*, put into Block Island to visit his mother and sisters, planning to rejoin Bellamy up in Maine.

Along with the *Whydah*, Bellamy's fleet included some smaller ships: the *Anne*—a galley-built snow taken off the capes of Virginia; the *Mary Anne*—a pink with more than 7,000 gallons of Madeira wine on board, captured early that morning; and the *Fisher*—a small sloop with a cargo of deer hides and tobacco, captured that afternoon.

There were 146 men on board the *Whydah*—130 pirates and 16 prisoners. The prisoners included the captains and some of the crew from the *Mary Anne* and the *Fisher*. Pirates split up captured crewmen, holding them in separate ships while they looted their vessels.

That very evening, April 26, 1717, a dense fog rolled in. Thunder rumbled. Lightning flashed. Waves began crashing over the deck …

An Arctic gale from Canada was colliding with a warm front moving northward from the Caribbean. Their confluence produced one of the worst storms ever to strike Cape Cod. Winds roared, kicking up huge waves that pounded the *Whydah*.

JOHN KING'S REMAINS

Forensic scientists have determined that this is the leg bone, or fibula, of a young boy. It was recovered from the wreck of the *Whydah* in the same concretion as this silk stocking and shoe. All three are most likely the remains of John King, the youngest member of Bellamy's pirate crew.

Abandon Hope, All Ye Who Enter Here

The nor'easter hit the *Whydah* at full force. The ship ran hard aground on a sandbar. The mainmast and other rigging snapped like twigs, and the *Whydah* rolled over. Some on board were swept over the side by the raging surf. Although the beach was just 500 feet away, the bitter ocean temperatures were cold enough to kill the strongest swimmer within minutes. Other crew members were crushed by the weight of falling rigging, cannon, and cargo as the ship, her treasure, and the remaining men on board plunged to the ocean floor, swallowed up by the shifting sands of the cape.

Of the 146 men aboard the *Whydah* that night, only two survived. Somehow Thomas Davis, the carpenter, and young John Julian managed to swim to shore and scale the steep sand cliffs. Davis found temporary refuge in the home of Cape Cod locals Samuel Harding and his wife, but he and Julian were soon picked up by the authorities.

SWALLOWED BY A STORM

Pages 128–129: Sam Bellamy drove the *Whydah* into a perfect storm, a warm front meeting a gale.

One of those who did not make it ashore was the young John King. He died pinned to the seabed by a cannon. A French woven-silk stocking and a boy's leather shoe that fastened with a buckle were all that he left behind. Both reflected 18th-century upper-class style, perhaps clues to the sort of family John King left behind when he turned pirate.

Found along with these artifacts was a fragment of a young person's leg bone, almost certainly that of John King. The rebellious boy who defied his mother to run off with the pirates met an early tragic death in the *Whydah* shipwreck.

The Fate of the Whydah's Consorts

When the storm hit, the *Mary Anne* likewise went aground, but Thomas Baker hacked down the foremast and mizzenmast, saving the ship from breaking up in the surf. The other two consorts—the *Anne* and the *Fisher*—suffered significant damage but rode out the storm.

The next morning, the four pirates aboard the *Fisher* joined their 19 crewmates on the *Anne*. With Richard Noland, the *Whydah*'s former quartermaster, in command, the pirates proceeded to Cape Elizabeth, Maine, where they hoped to rendezvous with Palgrave Williams on the *Marianne*, who had managed to miss the storm altogether.

Several *Whydah* crewmen had spent the night on the *Mary Anne*, including Hendrick Quintor. The pirates were devastated to learn of the loss of the *Whydah* and the disappearance of their crewmates. They knew they had to flee before the authorities arrived. They got to shore and set off together on foot, heading for Rhode Island, a famous pirate haunt. To fortify their spirits, they stopped off for an ill-conceived drink at Eastham Tavern, where they were soon arrested by the local deputy sheriff.

JOhN kING

On November 9, 1716, John King and his mother were sailing on board the *Bonetta* from Jamaica en route for Antigua when their ship was captured by Sam Bellamy. In a court disposition later recorded in Antigua, Abijah Savage, the commander of the *Bonetta,* describes how Bellamy and his men plundered the ship for 15 days and took John King along with them when they left. John King, Commander Savage insisted, was "so far from being forced or compelled" to join the pirates "that he declared he would kill himself if he was restrained, and even threatened his mother."

MAP OF THE AMERICAS, 1780

The importance of the Caribbean archipelago and the South and Central American coastline to voyagers and venturers in the Old World is revealed by their disproportionate size in this late 18th-century map.

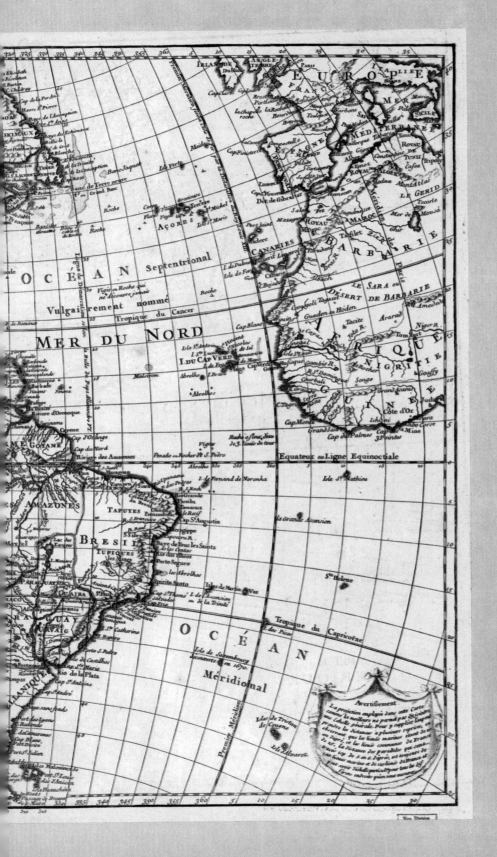

ANCHOR

Opposite: This anchor, one of the *Whydah's* smaller anchors, was likely used as a kedge anchor, rowed out from a ship already at anchor and used to turn the vessel about while in port.

HAWSER

The hawser is a large, heavy rope used to tow, moor, or secure a ship. Frayed rope would be repaired or replaced as currency in the slave trade.

Blind Justice

In colonial Boston, all trials were a form of public spectacle, but pirate trials generated particular excitement.

On October 18, 1717, after seven months cooped up in a dark prison cell, the captured survivors from the *Mary Anne* faced the full glare of a Boston courtroom. That day, there was standing room only as the seven defendants—still wearing the same clothes they had worn on the night of the storm—faced the judges.

The men were charged with piracy and robbery. The penalty was death by hanging. One at a time, seven survivors—Hendrick Quintor, Thomas South, Peter Cornelius Hoof, John Shaun, John Brown, Thomas Baker, and Simon Van Vorst—offered up the only defense they could. Each insisted he was forced to sign the ship's Articles; each swore that he had been pressed into piracy.

Thomas South was the only man acquitted. His six shipmates were found guilty and sentenced to death by hanging.

Cotton Mather—minister of Boston's Old North Church—was in the courtroom to hear the testimony and verdicts. A fire-and-brimstone preacher and prolific writer, Mather had entered Harvard at the age of 12 and had preached his first sermon at the age of 16. He was personally committed to persuading the pirates to repent. Throughout their months in jail, Mather regularly met with Bellamy's men.

On November 15, accompanied by Cotton Mather, the condemned men were rowed across the harbor to Charleston, where their gallows had been set up at the water's edge.

Apparently these meetings had some effect. All six men convicted of piracy repented—but still they hanged, the tide lapping their feet and the skyline of old Boston rising in the distance. Mather published the story of the trial and execution in a pamphlet called "The End of Piracy." Such booklets were common at the time. People liked to read the confessions of pirates and tales of justice being served. But Mather's title was ahead of its time. The trial of Bellamy's men wasn't the end of piracy. It would take another ten years for the pirates to be soundly defeated.

Tried separately from the *Mary Anne* pirates, Thomas Davis, the *Whydah* carpenter, survived the harsh justice of the Boston courtroom. Davis was tried separately from the *Mary Anne* pirates. The judges accepted his claim that he was an honest seaman, pressed into service by Bellamy's crew because they needed a carpenter. Thomas walked out of the Boston courtroom a free man.

John Julian was the only one of Bellamy's crew not to be tried. Like many other captured black and Native American pirates, the 16-year-old Miskito Indian was separated from his mates and sold into slavery.

Under the command of Richard Noland, the badly damaged *Anne* made it up to Cape Elizabeth, Maine. Having said good-bye to his mother and sisters in Block Island, Palgrave Williams showed up on the *Marianne* and took the 19 *Anne* pirates aboard with him. After a month of raiding the coasts of Massachusetts and New York, the crew met up with La Buse off Virginia. The pirates banded together and headed back down to their old haunt, New Providence, Bahamas.

The End of the "Golden Age of Piracy"

At the height of the age of piracy, there were around 2,000 pirates operating in the Caribbean and along the North American coast. That number might seem small until you compare it to population figures for several

COURT SCENE

Following pages: The trial of the crewmen from Bellamy's flotilla took place in Boston on October 18, 1717. The packed courtroom listened as the guilty verdicts were read out.

regional cities in 1700: New York City had 18,000 citizens; Charleston, South Carolina, had 5,000; and even Port Royal, Jamaica, had a population of 3,000.

Just imagine: Two thousand outlaws with nothing to lose, armed to the teeth, sailing in some of the best-equipped and most technologically advanced ships of their day, attacking people where they were most vulnerable and isolated—on board ship on the open sea.

Navies faced challenges trying to capture pirates. The distances to patrol were huge. They had few ships and little funds. Captains weren't authorized to buy supplies in the expensive Caribbean, nor allowed to stop long enough to careen their ships. The pirates, flush with money and in smaller, faster ships, were more familiar with the local waters. They could easily escape to shallow inlets and bays and lay low.

All through 1715 and 1716, the British Navy didn't capture a single pirate ship. In early 1717, one was taken off St. Croix, but the men aboard managed to escape. Some of those men were picked up by Sam Bellamy and joined his crew.

In 1717, the British authorities increased the number of warships they sent out in pursuit of pirates. And they announced rewards—substantial by the standards of the day— to seamen who apprehended pirates: 100 pounds sterling for a pirate captain, 40 pounds for an officer, and 20 pounds for a regular pirate.

In 1718, Woodes Rogers, a famous former privateer, was appointed governor of the Bahamas. His commission: to rid the Bahamas and New Providence of piracy. Rogers offered an amnesty: Swear off piracy, go straight, and all would be forgotten. He made it clear that anyone who chose to keep operating under the black flag would be captured, tried, and hanged. In response, many pirates accepted the amnesty. Others moved their area of operations.

RAMSHEAD BLOCK

A halyard would attach to the hook end of this pulley, lines to another block on the other, reducing the force needed to hoist sails and heavy objects.

By 1719, the number of pirates directly attacking slaving ships off the African coast had grown. Working in flotillas, some made up of more than 500 pirates under the command of several captains, they caused serious disruption to the slave trade. With their profits under threat, the British parliament acted aggressively to protect their interests. New antipiracy laws were passed in 1721, and Royal Navy warships were dispatched to capture or kill pirates on sight.

The veteran pirate captains Jennings and Hornigold—neither of whom had ever attacked British ships—opted for the 1718 pardon. Hornigold and Cockram took commissions from Woodes Rogers to hunt down pirates. Stede Bonnet was captured, put on trial, and hanged in Charleston, Massachusetts. Edward Teach—Blackbeard—originally surrendered under the amnesty, but soon he was back on the account. He was killed by a naval lieutenant in November 1718 in a spectacular shipboard battle. Two years later, Jack Rackham's crew—including Anne Bonny and Mary Read—were arrested and tried. Most of them were hanged. A few weeks later, Charles Vane, another veteran of New Providence, was captured, tried, and hanged.

Many pirates were killed in battle or were hanged. Hundreds of others accepted pardons. But hundreds escaped, blending into communities in colonial America, the Virgin Islands, Madagascar, and West Africa.

In 1722, Bart Roberts was killed by Capt. Challoner Ogle off the coast of West Africa. More than 50 of Black Bart's crew members were hanged from gallows set up along the coast. The death of Roberts was a major blow. It signaled the turning point in the war against the pirates.

By the end of 1723, more than a thousand pirates had been killed or captured. About 500 were hanged. In 1730, La Buse—the last of the pirates of the "Golden Age" still operating—was captured. He was hanged on the beach on the island of Bourbon in the Indian Ocean. The crowd cheered.

CHAINPLATE

Iron chainplates like this were used to secure rigging to the hull of the ship. They had to hold tight and withstand the force of strong winds against the sails that hung from tall wooden masts.

Pirates With Attitude

FIGHT TO THE FINISH

Blackbeard's final battle with the Royal Navy, dramatized in this painting by J. L. R. Ferris, became the stuff of legend. One tale even has the pirate's headless corpse swimming around his vanquisher's sloop several times. Myths aside, the slaying of Blackbeard was a major coup for the Navy.

Some pirates displayed genuine regret at their trials. Many others parroted the dramatic confessions they knew Cotton Mather and others wanted to hear. But there were other pirates who refused to show any remorse. These men stayed defiant to the end.

Some pirates remained steadfast about their choice of lifestyle. At his hanging in Boston in 1726, for example, William Fly didn't succumb to the coaching of Cotton Mather. Fly stood on the gallows and proclaimed that merchant captains were responsible for driving ordinary seamen into piracy by mistreating them and

refusing to pay them on time. Thomas Morris, hanged in the Bahamas in 1718, wished he'd been "a greater Plague to these Islands."

Others acted as if they cared little whether they lived or died. When they tried to hang John Gow in 1726, the rope broke. Gow simply picked himself up, nonchalantly brushed himself off, and climbed the ladder a second time to be hanged. Others, however, refused to surrender and blew themselves up rather than be captured and hanged.

Pirates' trials and executions were public spectacles, and sometimes the pirates played them for all they were worth. In 1717, a crowd in Kingston, Jamaica, rescued a pirate from the gallows. At a mass hanging of pirates in New Providence, Bahamas, many of the spectators were pirates themselves. The prisoners, playing to the audience, shouted out rebellious speeches as they went to their deaths.

Blackbeard's Last Stand

Blackbeard threatened to burn Boston to the ground if they hanged Bellamy's men. Only the timely arrival of a warship kept him from carrying out his threat. He instead attacked shipping from New England, burning the vessels he took in revenge. On November 22, 1718, Navy seamen led by Lt. Robert Maynard went after Blackbeard in two sloops hired by Governor Alexander Spotswood of Virginia. Maynard and his men found Blackbeard's sloop, the *Adventure,* anchored off sandbanks at Ocracoke Inlet, North Carolina.

Taking the pirates by surprise, the naval sailors engaged them in bloody hand-to-hand combat. A Scots Highlander on Maynard's crew swung his sword and lopped off Blackbeard's head. Maynard hung it as a trophy from the bow of his ship and sailed back to harbor with the surviving pirate crewmen on board. After their trial, all but two of Blackbeard's crew members were hanged.

REMAINS OF THE HULL

Huge chunks of shipwrecked remains strew the waters off the Massachusetts coast. As the *Whydah* rode through the storm, beaten by the wind and waves, she shattered beneath the weight of her cannon and rigging. Her remains spread out four miles underwater.

The End of Bart Roberts

Bart Roberts was still creating havoc on the West African coast. Capt. Challoner Ogle, aboard the H.M.S. *Swallow,* a two-deck warship with 50 guns, stalked the famous pirate captain for weeks. On February 5, 1722, Ogle and his crew caught up with Roberts's flotilla off Cape Lopez, Gabon. Roberts and his crew mistook the Navy warship for a rich merchantman.

Roberts sent one of his ships, under the command of James Skyrm, in pursuit of the *Swallow.* After drawing the pirates away from Roberts's flotilla, Ogle turned his guns on the ship. Skyrm had his leg blown off but fought on. It was a lost cause, however, and Ogle soon defeated and captured the pirates. They were taken back to port, and Ogle turned the *Swallow* back to Cape Lopez, intent on killing or capturing Roberts.

The captives were taken back to port in Africa. After that, Ogle turned the *Swallow* in the direction of Cape Lopez. No doubt he was intent on killing or capturing Roberts.

On February 10, Ogle arrived back at Cape Lopez. Roberts—looking every inch the pirate captain, wearing a crimson waistcoat and breeches, topped with a cap with a red feather—failed once again to recognize the *Swallow* as what it was: a Navy warship.

Most of his crewmates were drunk. Ogle turned his guns on the pirate flagship, the *Royal Fortune.* In the midst of the melee, Roberts received a fatal shot to the throat. Ogle quickly captured the remainder of Roberts's crew and managed to do so without sustaining a single casualty among the men aboard his own ship.

The 75 black men among Roberts's crew were sold into slavery. Some of the other pirates were sold into indentured servitude in the West African mines. All told, 52 of Roberts's crewmen were hanged.

DEADEYES

Deadeyes, made of hardwood, were used to secure the standing rigging that held up the mast. Ropes threaded through the deadeye's three holes, and the deadeye itself attached to the ship's hull with a chainplate.

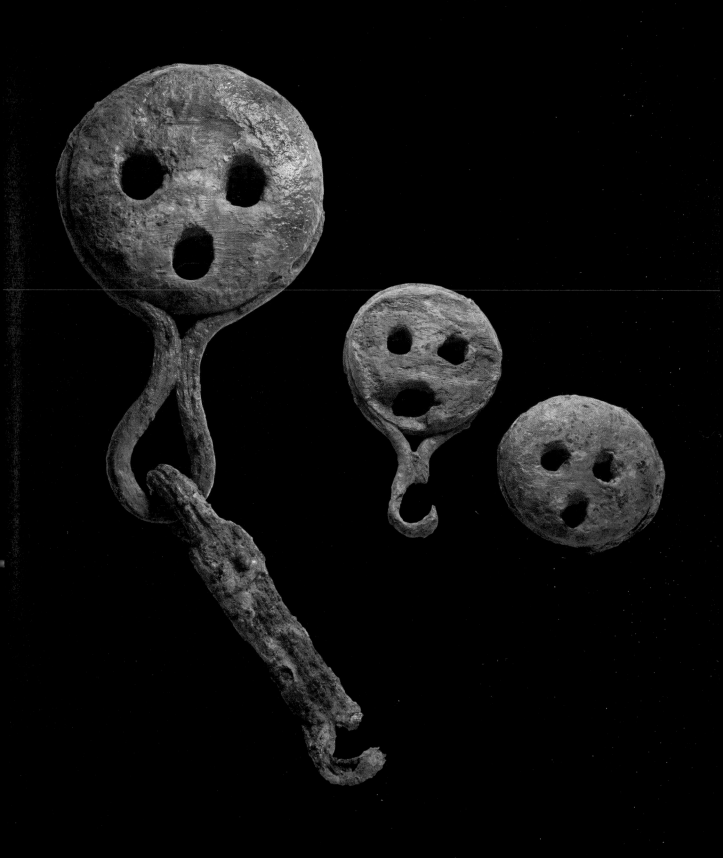

THE GIBBET

A device not to execute but to display already dead bodies—a gruesome warning for would-be pirates—the gibbet often stood on a prominent point at the entrance to a port. Pirate captains William Kidd and "Calico Jack" Rackham were both hanged and exhibited in gibbets.

A Pirate's Grisly Fate

The authorities on both sides of the Atlantic, in European nations and in their colonies of the New World, were determined to stamp out piracy. All the authorities came up with ways to do what they could to make examples of pirates, discouraging others from taking to the high seas.

Convicted pirates were hanged in public, in visible locations at the entrances to ports. Often they were executed in groups, and often under their own black flag. Pirates so loathed this practice that, when captured, many threw their flags overboard to prevent them from being hoisted in triumph over the gallows.

After they had been hanged, pirates' corpses were often cut down and covered in tar. They were then suspended in a metal cage called a gibbet and displayed for months, while their flesh slowly rotted. The macabre sight of groups of dangling men was a graphic warning to sailors of the perils of piracy. A decomposing body in a gibbet only reinforced that grisly message.

Before the 1500s, captured pirates were often secured alive with pegs on the banks of the Thames at Wapping in London at low tide. As the tide rose to cover them, the victims slowly drowned.

Authorities refused to bury pirates in cemeteries or other consecrated ground. Often they were buried on the beach, between the tidemarks. At the time people believed that if you weren't buried in consecrated ground, your soul was doomed to wander until Judgment Day—so the punishment served on a pirate lasted through all eternity.

The British, French, Dutch, Portuguese, and Spanish all hanged pirates. By the 1720s the Atlantic world was full of gallows. From Cape Coast Castle, Africa, to Antigua; from Boston to the Bahamas; from Cuba and Jamaica to London; and from Rhode Island to Salvador, Brazil, pirate bodies dangled on ropes at port entrances, a deterrent to all who might be tempted to go on the account.

The Legacy of the "Golden Age of Piracy"

... now and then we had a hope that, if we lived and were good, God would permit us to be pirates.

—Mark Twain

The pirates we know from movies and stories are fictional characters. But they are based on the stories of the real men who dominated the seas during the "Golden Age of Piracy." These men—and even a few women—lived on the margins of society in secret brotherhoods whose codes and practices we are only beginning to recognize and understand.

Our knowledge of real pirates is patchy. These men were rebels, not record-keepers. Most of what we know comes from their trials, from witnesses at their hangings, and from the testimony of people they robbed. That they could be ruthless, desperate, and bloodthirsty is without question.

Yet pirates also created a seaborne democracy when few on land had a voice, a vote, or any rights. They lived so large that the stories of their exploits continue to inspire writers, painters, dramatists, musicians, and filmmakers.

Who doesn't identify a little with Mark Twain's words?

Treasure Hunting

Under British law, once authorities recovered pirate loot, it belonged to the crown. Samuel Shute, the governor of Massachusetts, sent Capt. Cyprian Southack to Cape Cod to recover what he could from the *Whydah*. Southack was an experienced ship's captain and cartographer, or mapmaker. He was assigned

CORDAGE

With all the lines and rigging on an 18th-century sailing ship, the cordage represented great lengths of rope, manufactured of hemp, sisal, or other natural plant products.

to bring back "money, bullion, treasure, goods, and merchandize," as well as any surviving pirates that might be hiding out.

On his way from Boston, Southack's ship was attacked by pirates, who stole 80 pounds worth of supplies—an early omen for an ill-fated trip. Southack arrived at Cape Cod on May 2, 1717—a week after the wreck. All that was to be found on the beach were pieces of the ship that had washed ashore along with the remains of over a hundred dead pirates.

Southack found that the wreck itself was in water too rough, too deep, and too cold to make salvage possible. Anything of value was trapped inside the *Whydah*—the ship had rolled over and was breaking up as she sank into the sands.

Local people had stripped the shoreline clean, but Southack was determined not to return to Boston empty-handed. He placed a notice in the local paper

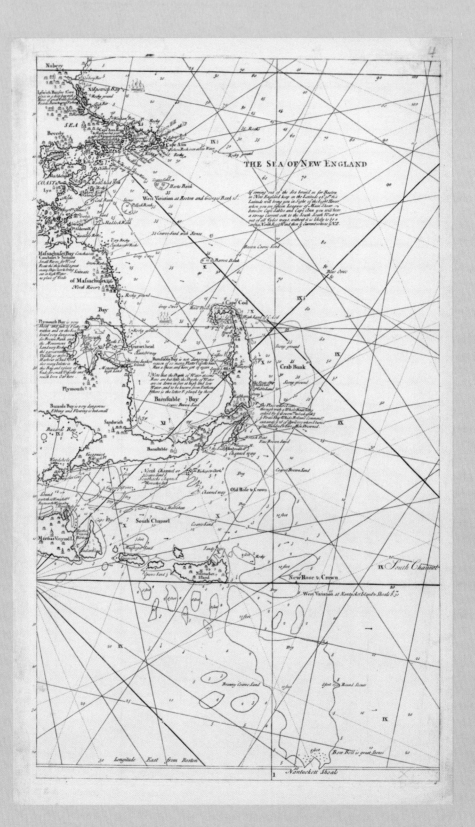

announcing his intention to search every house—breaking down doors, chests, or trunks if necessary—and seize any goods or pirates from the *Whydah* that he found. The search covered a 30-mile-wide radius from the wreck itself—and recovered absolutely nothing.

Southack sailed back to Boston with "two anchors, two great guns, and some junk." Although he didn't find the treasure, he made detailed notes and precise charts of his adventure. Almost 300 years later, Barry Clifford pieced these together and used them to determine the location of the wreck of the *Whydah*.

The riches, with the guns, would be buried in the sand.

—Capt. Cyprian Southack

Finding Buried Treasure

It's not what you find, it's what you find out.

—Barry Clifford

Almost 300 years after Sam Bellamy met his fate off Wellfleet, Barry Clifford set out to search for the *Whydah*. If not for Barry's determination and persistence, the story of Bellamy and the fate of the *Whydah* would have been one more shipwreck legend, the true story lost forever.

The hunt for the ship started in libraries. Research led to a number of historical documents, including Southack's map. Slowly a picture developed of how the geography of the region had changed over time. Combined with his own knowledge of the local waters, weather, and tides, Barry Clifford became convinced that he could locate the site of the *Whydah*.

Expedition Whydah

Understanding history is what the Expedition Whydah project is all about.

—Barry Clifford

What does it take to recover artifacts from a shipwreck like the *Whydah?* There are a number of answers to that question.

First, the work involves a crew of technicians, divers, deckhands, conservators, and archaeologists, dedicated to the job.

Next, the expedition needs a stable boat, rigged for dive support and underwater excavation. Diving equipment and dry suits, so divers can stay underwater for long periods, are essential. Because of the relatively shallow waters at the *Whydah* site, divers do not need to wear the kind of equipment needed in deeper wreck sites. But the water temperature in the North Atlantic around Cape Cod is always cold, so divers always need dry suits and sometimes even hot-water suits.

A number of tools are essential for the search, especially a magnetometer and other sensing gear to map the presence of metal in the area. To make sense of objects brought up from underwater and conserve the artifacts found on the site, an expedition needs a good lab.

And, perhaps most important of all, it takes stamina, motivation, and the grit to keep the project going. All of those things went into recovering the pieces, and the story, of the *Whydah,* the slave ship turned pirate ship.

A number of logistical problems presented themselves. The wreck was buried 10 to 30 feet in the sand beneath the seabed. The area, used as a test-firing range during World War II, was full of debris. More than 3,000 ships had sunk off Cape Cod in the past 400 years. How could Barry find one specific ship? On top of all that, Cape Cod weather is unpredictable. Violent storms rise up with no warning.

Undaunted by such obstacles, Barry Clifford and his team started work in 1983. At first, they came up empty-handed. But on July 23, 1984, a diver found the first possible evidence of the ship: a concreted cannon in the base of an excavation pit.

A year later, in the fall of 1985, the team made an essential discovery. They recovered the bell from the *Whydah*.

Now, finally, here it was—irrefutable proof that Barry Clifford and his team had located the fabled shipwreck.

DIVING FOR TREASURE

Following pages: Recovering items from the murky seas off the cape demands expertise and ingenuity. Divers must work hard to locate and remove objects before the sand sweeps back to cover them.

JFK JR.'S COMPASS

John F. Kennedy, Jr., was one of the original Expedition Whydah divers. In 1983 he lost his compass while diving at the site. Twenty-three years later the dive team recovered it, above, near the site of 15 concreted cannon.

Needle in a Haystack

Finding and mapping a shipwreck hundreds of years after the fact is a complicated task.

The *Whydah* is an "exploded site," meaning that the ship was shattered when it underwent the wreck. The vessel and her contents lay scattered across a wide area. To compound matters, the sand on the seafloor at Cape Cod blows and moves like a desert storm. The ship and her contents had been swallowed by the shifting sands.

The first step was to map anomalies across the site by towing a proton precision magnetometer across the suspected location. A magnetometer detects the presence of iron or steel. When it senses the presence of a metal, it records a "hit" on a graph in that area. The team meticulously charted the position of each hit on a large map of the site. Zones with a high concentration of hits became study areas.

The second step was establishing the underwater site as if it were an archaeological dig. Archaeologists establish a site on land in four steps:

1. Create borders using stakes and string and then lay a grid within the borders.

2. Draw a copy of the grid on paper.

3. Dig up each square within the grid, one square at a time, excavating objects.

4. On the paper grid, record the exact location of each object found within each square. Then assign a number to each object, photograph it, and write a detailed description of it.

HAMMER

From pieces of gold to ordinary tools, like this hammer, none of the artifacts from the *Whydah* has been sold. The collection remains intact, for further study and research.

X-Ray Visions

Thanks to state-of-the-art X-ray technology, Barry Clifford and the Expedition Whydah conservation team can see inside concretions before they begin the tedious and exacting process of removing the artifacts from the sediment and rock caked all around them. Working with Clifford's team, technology experts at Canon Medical Systems, a division of Canon U.S.A., Inc., found themselves looking into objects entirely different from what they usually view.

Traditional X-ray machines provide a flat, somewhat fuzzy image. Cutting-edge digital X-ray technology makes major improvements. The combination of a deployable X-ray generator with a portable digital radiography detector results in a system that can be brought to the objects of interest and result in sharp, high-quality, digital images gained through a minimally invasive procedure.

Two different systems were brought in to help Expedition Whydah. One was a larger, higher-powered mobile X-ray system of the type used in hospitals, powerful enough to be called an "X-ray room on wheels." Canon technicians trained this high-powered system at concretions in the conservation laboratories in Provincetown, Massachusetts. The other was a less powerful yet more portable machine—officially called a Field Deployable Digital Radiography System (FDDRS)—which is used in field operations such as disaster relief situations. This deployable system was brought aboard *Vast Explorer,* the expedition vessel, to view concretions just pulled up out of the water.

In some ways, the concretions pulled up from under the Cape Cod waters presented challenges tougher than those faced in a medical setting. Not only was the rock surrounding the artifacts of a higher density than tissue and bone, but everything in the concretion—surrounding rock and enclosed artifacts, made primarily of metal or wood—was of a similarly high density. The challenge faced by X-ray experts was to tweak the settings of the X-ray equipment in order to bring out the detail of the artifacts in contrast from the medium that surrounded them.

Expedition Whydah team members, who had cracked open many a concretion before, knew the telltale signs: the shape of coins or pistols, for example. They were able to point to details of interest, guiding X-ray operators in fine-tuning their visual results.

The results were fascinating, to *Whydah* explorers and Canon technicians alike.

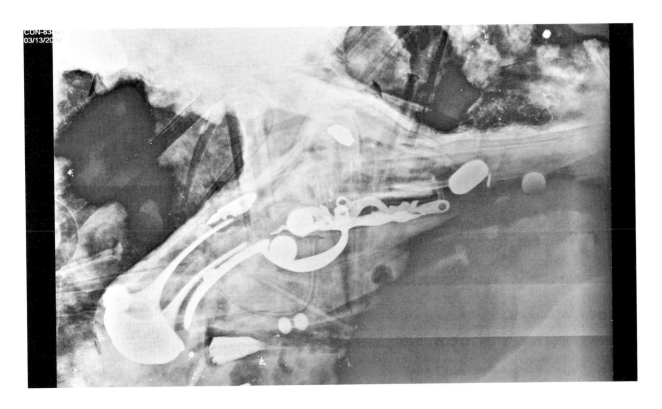

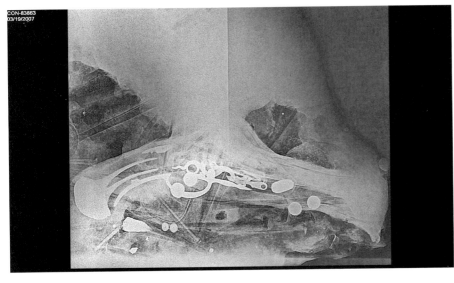

PISTOL REVEALED

X-ray imagery reveals that this concretion contains an elegant Sun King pistol—the second recovered so far from the *Whydah* site. One power *(above)* reveals the outline of metal parts. A higher power *(left)* uses edge enhancement to sharpen detail.

Opposite: *Whydah* conservators work on a tea kettle. For this artifact, as for all the others, they must determine a specific course of action to keep it from deteriorating further. Each item recovered presents its own challenges.

GUN PARTS BAG

Tools of a gunsmith's trade fuse into a three-dimensional collage. Metals in objects from the *Whydah* combine with salts in seawater to form a conglomerate that cements rock, sand, clay, and nearby artifacts together.

But you can't make a grid using string and pegs in turbulent waters with shifting sands, so archaeologists and conservators had to develop special underwater archaeological techniques to recover and record items as they were found.

To excavate an area of the site, team members drop three or more anchors, to securely position the ship in one place.

Then a device known as a mailbox is lowered over the stern of the expedition boat and fitted around the propellers. The mailbox redirects the boat's wake from the propellers toward the seabed. The wake from the propellers clears away the sand and exposes the artifacts.

Once the pit has been excavated, the dive team maps the position of larger objects, such as cannon. These are then hoisted onto the boat.

Next, divers use handheld metal detectors to locate smaller objects. They create a grid of the pit to help map such artifacts. They have to work very quickly, removing objects as fast as they can before the pit refills with sand.

Concretions

All of the objects that sank with the *Whydah* have remained underwater for centuries. Many are embedded in masses of material called concretions.

Metals submerged in seawater undergo electrolytic reactions. They start to disintegrate and combine with the salts that are present in ocean water.

The metals and the salts form a conglomerate that cements rock, sand, clay, and any other nearby artifacts into a mass. As long as the mass, or concretion, remains submerged in saltwater, most of the

objects inside stay relatively stable. But if the concretion is brought to the surface and allowed to dry out, the objects inside quickly deteriorate from the salts in the seawater soaked into them.

Whydah concretions go through a series of conservation steps, including electrolysis, to remove the artifacts from the concretions. The artifacts are carefully and individually conserved for study and display.

To remove an artifact from a concretion, the concretion must first be placed in a tank filled with fresh water. After two to four weeks, the concretion is moved to a tank filled with a chemical solution specific to that artifact. Low-voltage electricity is applied to the solution in a process known as electrolytic reduction. The length of time an artifact spends in the reduction bath depends on its composition, its size, and its condition. An artifact made of silver or

CONSERVING CANNON

Following pages: Artifacts are transported from the site to the Expedition Whydah lab. Here cannon are stored in seawater, to minimize chemical change before conservation can begin.

lead may take only a few days of weeks to undergo conservation, while an iron cannon may take anywhere from two to four years.

Salts that have accumulated in the artifact over time are slowly removed. The process also helps loosen stone, iron oxides, and other debris. Slowly, the artifact is exposed. Any remaining concretion is removed using picks, brushes, or air scribes, which shoot out a fine, targeted blast of air. The artifact is thoroughly washed and dried and, finally, covered with a protective sealant.

Small concretions were found among the remains of the *Whydah* as well. One was a tea kettle, a utensil highly valued by pirates out on the salty seas for weeks or months at a time. The base of the *Whydah*'s large kettle was shaped to fit in a recess of the ship's stove to prevent it from toppling over in heavy seas.

Not only was tea or coffee a pleasant treat, but water stored on board a ship like the *Whydah* soon became contaminated with microorganisms. If the water wasn't thoroughly boiled, it could result in deadly outbreaks of diseases such as typhoid.

Another smaller concretion formed around a hemp bag, full of gun parts, which probably belonged to the armorer on board the *Whydah*.

Conserving the Artifacts

Conservators apply their scientific training to remove artifacts from concretions and to prevent the further deterioration of the artifacts. They determine the appropriate procedures to follow, including which chemical solutions to use, the concentrations of those solutions, and the voltage and wattage of the electricity to be applied in the electrolytic bath.

Conservators make their decisions on a case-by-case basis, supported by their knowledge of how different materials react when placed in a range of chemical solutions. Once the process of deconcretion and conservation begins, it is constantly monitored and adjusted. After an artifact has been thoroughly de-concreted, a chemical coating protects it from further decay.

Conservators use many specialized tools to carry out their work. Here are some examples of their tools:

- Pneumatic air scribes are an aggressive but effective way to remove artifacts from especially hard concretions. Their use requires considerable skill.
- Dental picks and dissecting tools are used for fine work when conservators need to work slowly and carefully to remove remaining concretions.
- To avoid scratching the artifacts, conservators use soft-bristled brushes to remove any remaining loose pieces of concretion.
- Glass lab equipment allows conservators to mix and measure the chemicals needed in conservation.
- Chemicals are used to create a variety of solutions. Some examples are polyethylene glycol (PEG), sodium hydroxide, and sodium sesquicarbonate.
- A stir plate is often used to quickly create a uniform solution.

FINESSE

Once artifacts are removed from a concretion, fine tools and a delicate touch are essential, to remove any remaining debris.

WELL-ARMED WHYDAH

By now many cannon have been recovered from the Whydah. Recent finds come from the storage area of the ship, between decks, where most of the cannon and perhaps the bulk of the ship's treasure were stored.

Seeing Inside a Concretion

Experience can hone the skill of "reading" a concretion. The overall shape of the concretion gives a hint of what's inside. For a more precise idea of the contents of a concretion, without awaiting the results of the slow process of electrolysis, cutting-edge imaging technology has much to offer. Using a miniature camera called a "lipstick camera," for example, Barry Clifford and his team were able to look inside a cannon before it was conserved.

Two cannon found on the *Whydah* were the 18th-century equivalent of modern safety deposit boxes. The guns were fitted with special plugs, hammered an inch or more into the barrels and sealed with pitch—and they were stuffed full of treasure. Other cannon loaded with pirate treasure have been found in different locations in the Caribbean.

Modern-Day Pirate Treasure

Unlike Bellamy's, there is, as of yet, no end to my story. Even though I have searched for sunken ships all over the world, I am always drawn back to the Whydah.

—Barry Clifford

Barry Clifford had dreamed of finding a pirate ship. He found that, and more—and he is still searching. Expedition *Whydah* is an ongoing project. Each diving season, Barry and his team return to the site and make new discoveries. Barry's passion for the project has not waned with time. The team continues to make use of technological advances to find more artifacts from the shipwreck. Each object reveals a little more about the life of pirates on the high seas.

THE QUEST CONTINUES

Following pages: Gazing out over the familiar seascape of Cape Cod, Barry Clifford found a pirate ship—and a never ending archaeological adventure.

Exhibition Credits

Real Pirates: The Untold Story of the *Whydah* from Slave Ship to Pirate Ship

A National Geographic Exhibition

PROJECT WHYDAH

Barry and Margot Clifford
Brandon Clifford
Lt. Cmdr. Alejandro Barrios
Dr. James Bradley
John de Bry
Robert Cembrola
Sean Graham
Bernie Heinze
Scott Herber
Kenneth J. Kinkor
Bob Lazier
Glen MacDonald
Derek McDonald
Todd Murphy
James Nelson
Jeff and Wesley Spiegel
Allan Tufankjian
Andris Zobs

ARTS AND EXHIBITIONS INTERNATIONAL

John Norman, President and Executive Producer
Mark Lach, Senior VP and Artistic Director
Michael Sampliner, COO
Brian Harris, VP Communications and Marketing
Christina Wright, Project Manager
Richard Bright, Production Manager
Jennifer Pawlikowsky, Marketing
Jason Simmons, General Manager

NATIONAL GEOGRAPHIC SOCIETY

Terry Garcia, Executive Vice President
Mission Programs

Betty Hudson, Executive Vice President
Communications

Sarah Laskin, Vice President
Mission Programs

Mimi Koumanelis, Director of Communications

Kathryn Keane, Director
Traveling Exhibitions Development

Mimi Koumanelis, Director
Communications

Ford Cochran
Mission Programs Online

Susan Norton, Director
NG Museum

CINCINNATI MUSEUM CENTER

Doug McDonald, Director
Dr. John Fleming, Vice President for Museums

EXHIBITION CONTENT, DESIGN AND INSTALLATION

Sharon Simpson, Exhibition Writer
SJS Projects

Tom Fricker, Exhibition Designer
Fricker Studio

David Dailing, Artifact Supervisor

Gregory Manchess, Illustrator

Margaret B. Stogner, Media Production
Blue Bear Films

Kenneth L. Garrett, Photography

David Mauk, Music Composition

Rick Belzer, Lighting Designer

Sam Rembert, Lighting

Ellen Przybyla
Alan Sprecher
Kenny Warren

ARTIFACT INSTALLATION

Lexington Studios, Exhibition Production
Richard and Frank Bencivengo
Howard Smith
Richard Bizzy
Jerry Parra
John Hogg

Hunt Design Associates, Graphic Design
Heather Watson

Crush Creative, Graphic Production
John Gibson

Edwards Technologies, Audio and Video
Brian Edwards, John Brandt

Joe Powell, Case Production
Benosh Productions

Canon Medical Systems, Canon U.S.A., Inc.
Whit Fowler and Greg Dice

GE Aviation QT NDE Services
Matt Prefontaine, Graphics
Alan Parente, Graphics

ADVISORY PANEL

Dr. Thomas C. Battle, Director
Moorland-Spingarn Research Center
Howard University

Dr. Ira Berlin, Distinguished University Professor
Department of History
University of Maryland

Dr. W. Jeffrey Bolster, Professor
Early American, Caribbean History
University of New Hampshire

Mr. Michael Cottman, Senior Correspondent
Reach Media, Inc.
President, Black Scuba Divers Association

Dr. Laurent Dubois, Associate Professor of History
Michigan State University

Dr. Wendy Wilson Fall, Associate Professor
Department of Pan African Studies
Kent State University

Dr. John Fleming, Vice President for Museums
Cincinnati Museum Center

Dr. Robert L. Harris, Jr., Vice-Provost
Cornell University

Dr. Marcus Rediker, Professor of History
University of Pittsburgh

Dr. Faith Ruffins, Curator
Division of Home and Community Life
Smithsonian Institution

Dr. Michael Washington, Chair
African Studies Department
Northern Kentucky University

Dr. Francille Rusan Wilson, Chair
African American Studies Department
University of Maryland

References and Reading

W. Jeffrey Bolster, *Black Jacks: African American Seamen in the Age of Sail*. Cambridge: Harvard University Press, 1998.

Barry Clifford with Paul Perry, *Expedition Whydah: The Story of the World's First Excavation of a Pirate Treasure Ship and the Man Who Found Her*. New York: Harper Collins, 1999.

David Cordingly, *Under the Black Flag: The Romance and Reality of Life Amongst the Pirates*. New York: Random House, 2006.

David Cordingly, ed., *Pirates: Terror on the High Seas from the Caribbean to the South China Sea*. North Dighton, MA: World Publications Group, 1998.

Daniel Defoe, *A General History of the Pyrates*. New York: Dover, 1999.

George Francis Dow and John Henry Edmonds, *The Pirates of the New England Coast (1630-1730)*. New York: Dover, 1996.

Peter Earle, *The Pirate Wars*. London: Methuen, 2003.

Olaudah Equiano, *The Interesting Narrative and Other Writings*. New York: Penguin, 2003.

Alexander O. Exquemelin. *The Buccaneers of America*. New York: Dover, 2000.

Robert Harms, *The Diligent: A Voyage Through the Worlds of the Slave Trade*. New York: Basic Books, 2003.

Robin Law, *Ouidah: Social History Of a West African Slaving 'Port.'* Athens: Ohio University Press, 2004.

Peter Linebaugh and Marcus Rediker, *The Many-Headed Hydra: The Hidden History of the Revolutionary Atlantic*. New York: Beacon, 2001.

Colin A. Palmer, *Human Cargoes: The British Slave Trade to Colonial America, 1700-1739*. Chicago: University of Illinois, 1981.

The Pirates Own Book: Authentic Narratives of the Most Celebrated Sea Robbers. New York: Dover, 1993.

Marcus Rediker, *Villains of All Nations: Atlantic Pirates in the Golden Age*. New York: Beacon, 2005.

Elizabeth Reynard, *The Narrow Land: Folk Chronicles of Old Cape Cod*. Chatham, MA: Chatham Historical Society, 1985.

Frank Sherry, *Raiders and Rebels: The Golden Age of Piracy*. New York: Backinprint.com, 2000.

William Snelgrave, *A New Account of Some Parts of Guinea, and the Slave Trade*. London: Routledge, 1971.

Donovan Webster. "Pirates of the Whydah," NATIONAL GEOGRAPHIC, May 1999, Vol. 195, No. 5.

Websites of Interest

Captive Passage: The Transatlantic Slave Trade and the Making of the Americas. The Mariner's Museum. http://www.mariner.org/captivepassage/index.html/

Documenting the American South. University Library, University of North Carolina. http://docsouth.unc.edu/

Expedition Whydah. Whydah Museum, Provincetown, Mass. http://www.whydah.com

Lest We Forget: The Triumph Over Slavery. New York Public Library, The Schomburg Center. http://digital.nypl.org/lwf/english/site/flash.html/

National Maritime Museum. http://www.nmm.ac.uk/

National Underground Freedom Railroad. http://www.freedomcenter.org/index.html/

Transatlantic Slavery. Merseyside Maritime Museum. http://www.liverpoolmuseums.org.uk/maritime/slavery/index.asp

Illustrations Credits

All images are by Kenneth Garrett except for the following:

Cover: Permission of Harvard Map Collection, Harvard College Library; 4-5, Jean Nicolas Bellin/CORBIS; 6, Brian Skerry; 12-13, Gregory Manchess; 15, Library of Congress/Geography and Maps Division; 17, Gregory Manchess; 18-19, Getty Images; 20, Leonardo de Selva/CORBIS; 22, Courtesy of Jennifer Oram and Joan Pope; 24-25, Library of Congress; 28-29, The Mariners' Museum, Newport News, VA; 30, National Maritime Museum, London; 33, Schomburg Center; 34-35, Schomburg Center; 38, Olaudah Equiano alias Gustavus Vassa, a slave, 1789 (mezzotint)/British Library, London, UK, © British Library Board. All Rights Reserved/The Bridgeman Art Library; 40-41, Gregory Manchess; 43, Baldwin H. Ward & Kathryn C. Ward/CORBIS; 45, Gregory Manchess; 46, Map of the Island of Haiti, 1789 (coloured engraving), French School, (18th century)/Private Collection, Archives Charmet/The Bridgeman Art Library; 49, Frederick Judd Waugh/Getty Images; 50-51, National Maritime Museum, London; 56-57, Arne Hodalic/CORBIS; 60-61, National Maritime Museum, London; 72-73, Marooned, 1909 (oil on canvas), Pyle, Howard (1853-1911)/Delaware Art Museum, Wilmington, USA, Museum Purchase/The Bridgeman Art Library; 77, Which Shall Be Captain?, from 'The Buccaneers', published in Harper's Monthly Magazine, 1911 (oil on canvas), Pyle, Howard (1853-1911)/Delaware Art Museum, Wilmington, USA, Gift of Dr James Stillman/The Bridgeman Art Library; 78-79, Gregory Manchess; 83, Gregory Manchess; 84, CORBIS; 85, Hulton Archive/Getty Images; 86 (UP), Library of Congress; 86 (CTR), Library of Congress; 86 (LO), Library of Congress; 90-91, 'Alas!', pirates watching their quarry sail away, 1909 (colour litho) by Bernard Finegan Gribble (1873-1962) (after) ©Bibliotheque des Arts Decoratifs, Paris, France/Archives Charmet/The Bridgeman Art Library; 96, Stefano Bianchetti/CORBIS; 102-103, CORBIS; 108-109, So the Treasure was Divided, from 'The Fate of Treasure Town' by Howard Pyle, published in Harper's Monthly Magazine, December 1905 (oil on canvas), Pyle, Howard (1853-1911) / Delaware Art Museum, Wilmington, USA, Howard Pyle Collection/The Bridgeman Art Library; 114-115, Rare Book Department, Free Library of Philadelphia; 122 (LO), Brian Skerry; 125, Brian Skerry/NG Image Collection; 126, Blue Lantern Studio/CORBIS; 128-129, Gregory Manchess; 133, Gregory Manchess; 134-135, Library of Congress; 138-139, Gregory Manchess; 142, Bettmann/CORBIS; 144-145, Brian Skerry/NG Image Collection; 148, Hanging a pirate in a cage on high ground overlooking the sea (engraving), English School, (18th century)/Private Collection, Peter Newark Pictures/The Bridgeman Art Library; 152, Permission of Harvard Map Collection, Harvard College Library; 155, Brian Skerry/Image Collection; 156-157, Brian Skerry/Image Collection; 161 (UP), Canon Medical Systems; 161 (LO), Canon Medical Systems.

About the Authors

The author of five books on his shipwreck explorations off the coast of the United States, Venezuela, Madagascar, and Haiti, Barry Clifford is a Fellow of the Explorers' Club, a Rolex-Lowell Thomas awardee for his achievements in underwater archaeology, and an Explorer-in-Residence for the American Museum of Natural History. He made world headlines in 1984 with his discovery of the *Whydah*. Treasures from this shipwreck, still being recovered, are showcased at Clifford's Whydah Museum in Provincetown, Massachusetts.

For the past 20 years, Kenneth J. Kinkor has been director of research for underwater explorer Barry Clifford. He is the director of the Expedition Whydah Sea Lab and Learning Center in Provincetown, Massachusetts, where selected artifacts from the pirate shipwreck *Whydah* are displayed, and has served as the consulting historian for traveling displays of this collection. Kinkor lectures and writes on New England's colonial maritime history and has conducted editorial work and historical research for a wide variety of media.

Sharon Simpson is a writer and producer who works with a wide range of informal educational institutions and media organizations including museums, science centers, and large-format movie companies. She lives in New York City.

About the Photographer

Kenneth Garrett is an independent photographer who specializes in archaeology, paleontology, and ancient cultures worldwide. His photographs have appeared in magazines including NATIONAL GEOGRAPHIC, *Smithsonian, Forbes, Time,* and *Life,* and in numerous books including the recent National Geographic titles *Tutankhamun and the Golden Age of the Pharaohs* and *Hidden Treasures of Ancient Egypt.*

Real Pirates

by Barry Clifford and Kenneth J. Kinkor
with Sharon Simpson, Photography by Kenneth Garrett

**PUBLISHED BY THE
NATIONAL GEOGRAPHIC SOCIETY**

John M. Fahey, Jr., President and Chief Executive Officer
Gilbert M. Grosvenor, Chairman of the Board
Nina D. Hoffman, Executive Vice President;
   President, Book Publishing Group

PREPARED BY THE BOOK DIVISION

Kevin Mulroy, Senior Vice President and Publisher
Leah Bendavid-Val, Director of Photography Publishing and Illustrations
Marianne R. Koszorus, Director of Design

Barbara Brownell Grogan, Executive Editor
Elizabeth Newhouse, Director of Travel Publishing
Carl Mehler, Director of Maps

STAFF FOR THIS BOOK

Susan Tyler Hitchcock, Project and Text Editor
Peggy Archambault, Art Director
Dana Chivvis, Illustrations Editor
Michael Horenstein, Production Project Manager
Marshall Kiker, Illustrations Specialist
Al Morrow, Design Assistant

Jennifer A. Thornton, Managing Editor
Gary Colbert, Production Director

MANUFACTURING AND QUALITY MANAGEMENT

Christopher A. Liedel, Chief Financial Officer
Phillip L. Schlosser, Vice President
John T. Dunn, Technical Director
Chris Brown, Director
Maryclare Tracy, Manager
Nicole Elliott, Manager

Founded in 1888, the National Geographic Society is one of the largest nonprofit scientific and educational organizations in the world. It reaches more than 285 million people worldwide each month through its official journal, NATIONAL GEOGRAPHIC, and its four other magazines; the National Geographic Channel; television documentaries; radio programs; films; books; videos and DVDs; maps; and interactive media. National Geographic has funded more than 8,000 scientific research projects and supports an education program combating geographic illiteracy.

For more information, please call
1-800-NGS LINE (647-5463)
or write to the following address:

National Geographic Society
1145 17th Street N.W.
Washington, D.C. 20036-4688 U.S.A.

Visit us online at www.nationalgeographic.com/books

For information about special discounts
for bulk purchases, please contact
National Geographic Books Special Sales:
ngspecsales@ngs.org

For rights or permissions inquiries, please contact
National Geographic Books Subsidiary Rights:
ngbookrights@ngs.org

Library of Congress Cataloging-in-Publication Data available upon request.
ISBN: 978-1-4262-0262-9
Printed in U.S.A.

Real Pirates: The Untold Story of the *Whydah* from Slave Ship to Pirate Ship is organized by National Geographic and Arts and Exhibitions International (AEI), LLC, in cooperation with Cincinnati Museum Center.